THE NEW
CHICKEN
COOKBOOK

THE NEW
CHICKEN
COOKBOOK

THE VERY BEST POULTRY AND GAME RECIPES

CONSULTANT EDITOR
LINDA FRASER

ANNESS
PUBLISHING

ISBN 0–8317–1873–0

Editorial Director: Joanna Lorenz
Project Editor: Linda Fraser
Designers: Tony Paine and Roy Prescott
Photographers: Steve Baxter, Karl Adamson and Amanda Heywood
Food for Photography: Wendy Lee, Jane Stevenson and Elizabeth Wolf Cohen
Props Stylists: Blake Minton and Kirsty Rawlings
Additional recipes: Carla Capalbo and Laura Washburn

Printed and bound in Singapore

 The apple symbol indicates a low fat, low cholesterol recipe.

CONTENTS

Poultry Preparation – Tips and Techniques

Chicken and other birds are a mainstay of weekday meals, holiday gatherings and festive occasions. Knowing how to handle poultry helps you to make the most of it. Here we give you all the information you need from trussing and roasting through to preparing perfect stocks and sauces.

Trussing Poultry

Trussing holds a bird together during cooking so that it keeps a neat, attractive shape. If the bird is stuffed, trussing prevents the stuffing falling out. You can truss with strong string or with poultry skewers.

1 **For an unstuffed bird**: set it breast down and pull the flap of neck skin over the neck opening. Turn the bird breast up and fold each wing tip back, over the neck skin, to secure firmly behind the shoulder.

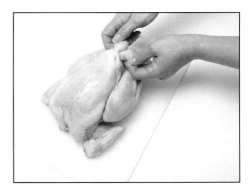

2 Press the legs firmly down and into the breast. If there is a band of skin across the parson's nose, fold back the ends of the drumsticks and tuck them under the skin.

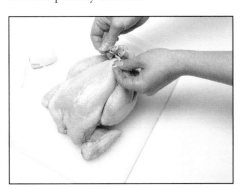

3 Otherwise, cross the knuckle ends of the drumsticks or bring them tightly together. Loop a length of string several times around the drumstick ends, then tie a knot and trim off the excess string.

4 **For a stuffed bird**: fold the wing tips back as above. After stuffing the neck end, fold the flap of skin over the opening and secure it with a skewer, then fold over the wing tips.

5 Put any stuffing or flavorings (herbs, lemon halves, apple quarters and so on) in the body cavity, then secure the ends of the drumsticks as above, tying in the parson's nose, too.

6 Alternatively, the cavity opening can be closed with skewers: insert two or more skewers across the opening, threading them through the skin several times.

7 Lace the skewers together with string. Tie the drumsticks together over the skewers.

Stuffing tips

When stuffing poultry, the stuffing should be cool, not hot or chilled. Pack it loosely into the bird because it will expand during cooking. Cook any left-over stuffing separately in a baking dish. Do not stuff poultry until just before putting it into the oven or pot. It is not a good idea to stuff the body cavity of a large bird because the stuffing could inhibit heat penetration, and thus not kill all harmful bacteria.

ROASTING POULTRY

Where would family gatherings be without the time-honored roast bird? But beyond the favorite chicken, all types of poultry can be roasted – from small Cornish hens to large turkeys. However, older, tougher birds are better pot-roasted.

SIMPLE ROAST CHICKEN

Squeeze the juice from a halved lemon over a 3-3½lb chicken, then push the lemon halves into the body cavity. Smear ½oz softened butter over the breast. Roast in a 375°F oven for about 1¼ hours. Skim all fat from the roasting juices, then add ½ cup water and bring to a boil, stirring well to mix in the browned bits. Season with salt and pepper, and serve this sauce with the chicken. *Serves 4.*

PROTECT AND FLAVOR

Before roasting, loosen the skin on the breast by gently easing it away from the flesh with your fingers. Press in softened butter – mixed with herbs or garlic for extra flavor – and carefully smooth back the skin.

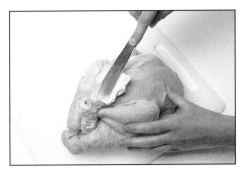

1 Wipe the bird inside and out with damp paper towels. Stuff the bird if the recipe directs and truss it. Spread the breast of chicken with softened or melted butter or oil; bard the breast of a lean game bird; prick the skin of duck and goose.

2 Set the bird breast-up on a rack in a small roasting pan or shallow baking dish. If you are roasting a lean game bird, set the bird in the pan breast down.

3 Roast the bird, basting it every 10 minutes after the first ½ hour with the accumulated juices and fat in the pan. Turn if directed. If browning too quickly, cover loosely with foil.

4 Transfer the bird to a carving board and leave to rest for at least 15 minutes before serving. During that time, make a simple sauce or gravy with the juices in the pan.

ROASTING TIMES FOR POULTRY

Note: Cooking times given here are for unstuffed birds. For stuffed birds, add 20 minutes to the total roasting time.

Cornish hen	1-1½lb	1-1¼ hours at 350°F
Chicken (broiler-fryer	2½-3lb	1-1¼ hours at 375°F
or roaster)	3½-4lb	1¼-1¾ hours at 375°F
	4½-5lb	1½-2 hours at 375°F
	5-6lb	1¾-2½ hours at 375°F
Duck (domestic)	3-5lb	1¾-2¼ hours at 400°F
Goose	8-10lb	2½-3 hours at 350°F
	10-12lb	3-3½ hours at 350°F
Turkey *(whole bird)*	6-8lb	3-3½ hours at 325°F
	8-12lb	3-4 hours at 325°F
	12-16lb	4-5 hours at 325°F
Turkey *(whole breast)*	4-6lb	1½-2¼ hours at 325°F
	6-8lb	2¼-3¼ hours at 325°F

PREPARING DUCK AND GOOSE FOR ROASTING

Duck and goose are bony birds, with most of their rich meat in the breast. There is a thick layer of fat under the skin which should be removed before cooking or melted out during cooking.

LEAN BY NATURE

Wild duck and geese are not as fatty as domestic birds, and should be prepared as you would a game bird so the meat doesn't dry out: bard the breast with bacon.

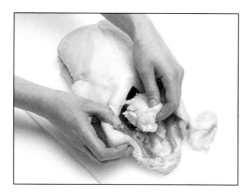

1 Pull out any fat from the body and neck cavities. Prick the skin all over the breast of the bird.

2 Tie the ends of the drumsticks together with string as for a chicken.

CARVING POULTRY

Carving a bird neatly for serving makes the presentation attractive. You will need a sharp, long-bladed knife, or an electric knife, plus a long two-pronged fork and a carving board with a well to catch the juices.

Cut away any trussing string. For a stuffed bird, spoon the stuffing from the cavity into a serving dish. For easier carving, remove the wishbone.

Insert the fork into one breast to hold the bird steady. Cut through the skin to the leg joint on that side of the body, then slice through it to sever the leg from the body. Repeat on the other side.

1 Slice through the joint in each leg to sever the thigh and drumstick. If carving turkey, slice the meat off the thigh and drumstick, parallel to the bone, turning to get even slices; leave chicken thighs and drumsticks whole.

2 To carve the breast of a turkey or chicken, cut ⅛–¼in thick slices at an angle, slicing down on both sides of the breastbone. For smaller birds, remove the meat on each side of the breastbone in a single piece, then slice thinly across the grain.

PREPARING TURKEY CUTLETS

Cutlets are slices cut crosswise from the turkey breast. Economical and extremely versatile, they are a lean meat that cooks quickly and can be used as a substitute in most recipes that call for veal scallopine. Turkey cutlets can also be treated in much the same way as thin beef or pork steaks, or used in place of chicken breast fillets.

Slicing across the grain ensures that the cutlet won't shrink or curl when it is cooked, and cutting on the diagonal gives good-sized slices.

1 With a large sharp knife, cut the boned breast across the grain, at a slight angle, into ⅜in slices.

2 Put each slice between two sheets of wax paper and pound lightly with the base of a pan to flatten.

BONING CHICKEN AND TURKEY BREASTS

Boneless poultry breasts, both whole and halves, are widely available, but they tend to be more expensive than bone-in breasts. So it is more economical to bone the breasts yourself, and it is really very easy to do. A thin-bladed boning knife is the ideal tool to use.

STOCKPILING BONES

Save chicken and other poultry bones in the freezer until you are ready to make stock. Store them up until you have enough.

1 **To take two boneless breast halves from a whole breast:** first pull off the skin and any loose fat. Then with the knife, cut through the breast meat along both sides of the ridged top of the breastbone.

2 With the knife at an angle, scrape the meat away from the bone down one side of the rib cage. Do this carefully so the breast meat comes away in one neat piece. Repeat on the other side. You now have two skinless boneless breast halves.

3 **To remove the meat from a breast half:** if the wing is attached, cut through the joint to separate the wing and breast. (Keep the wing for stock or another use.) Pull off the skin, if desired.

4 Turn the breast over and scrape the meat from the bone, using short strokes and lifting away the bone as it is freed.

5 Before cooking, remove the tendon next to the long flap or fillet on the underside of the breast. Cut it free of the meat at one end and pull it away, scraping it gently with the knife to remove it neatly.

6 Trim any fat from the breast. Put it between two sheets of plastic wrap or wax paper and pound lightly with a meat pounder, the base of a heavy pan or a rolling pin to flatten the breast slightly.

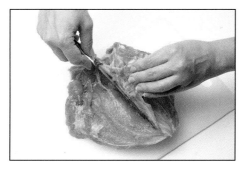

7 **To bone a whole breast for stuffing:** you must keep the skin intact. Set the breast skin-side down and scrape the meat away from the ribcage, starting at one side and working up to the ridged top of the breastbone. Repeat on the other side.

8 When the meat has been freed on both sides, lift up the ribcage and scrape the skin gently away from both sides of the top of the breastbone, taking care not to cut through the skin. The breast is now boned in one piece.

CUTTING UP POULTRY

Although chickens and other poultry are sold already cut up, sometimes it makes sense to buy a whole bird and to do the job yourself. That way you can prepare four larger pieces or eight smaller ones, depending on the recipe, and you can cut the pieces so the backbone and other bony bits (which can be saved for stock) are not included. In addition, a whole bird is cheaper to buy than pieces.

A sharp knife and sturdy kitchen scissors or poultry shears make the job of jointing poultry very easy.

SAFE HANDLING OF RAW POULTRY

Raw poultry may harbor potentially harmful organisms, such as salmonella bacteria, so it is vital to take care in its preparation. Always wash your hands, the chopping board, knife and poultry shears in hot soapy water before and after handling poultry. It is a good idea to use a chopping board that can be washed in a dishwasher and, if possible, to keep the chopping board just for the preparation of raw poultry. Thaw frozen poultry completely before cooking.

1 With the sharp knife, cut through the skin on one side of the body down to where the thigh joins the body. Bend the leg out away from the body and twist it to break the joint.

3 To separate the breast from the back, cut through the flap of skin just below the rib cage, cutting toward the neck. Pull the breast and back apart and cut through the joints that connect them on each side. Reserve the back for stock.

5 Cut the breast lengthwise in half, cutting through the wishbone. You now have two breasts with wings attached and two leg portions.

2 Hold the leg out away from the body and cut through the joint, taking the 'oyster' meat from the backbone with the leg. Repeat on the other side.

4 Turn the whole breast over, skin side down. Take one side of the breast in each hand and bend back firmly so the breastbone pops free. Loosen the bone on both sides with your fingers and, with the help of the knife, remove it.

6 For eight pieces, cut each breast in half at an angle so that some breast meat is included with a wing portion. Trim off any protruding bones.

7 With the knife, cut each leg portion through the joint to separate the thigh and drumstick.

MAKING POULTRY STOCK

A good homemade poultry stock is invaluable in the kitchen. It is simple and economical to make, and can be stored in the freezer for up to six months. If giblets are available, add them (except the livers) with the wings.

Makes about 2¹/₂ quarts

2¹/₂–3lb poultry wings, backs and necks (from chicken, turkey, etc)
2 onions, unpeeled and quartered
4 quarts cold water
2 carrots, roughly chopped
2 celery stalks, with leaves if possible, roughly chopped
a small handful of fresh parsley
a few fresh thyme sprigs or ³/₄ tsp dried thyme
1 or 2 bay leaves
10 black peppercorns, lightly crushed

1 Combine the poultry wings, backs and necks and the onions in a stockpot. Cook over moderate heat, stirring occasionally so they color evenly, until lightly browned.

2 Add the water and stir well to mix in the sediment on the bottom of the pot. Bring to a boil and skim off the impurities as they rise to the surface of the stock.

3 Add the remaining ingredients. Partly cover the stockpot and gently simmer the stock for 3 hours.

4 Strain the stock into a bowl and leave to cool, then chill.

A FRUGAL STOCK

Stock can be made from the bones and carcasses of roasted poultry, cooked with vegetables and flavorings. Save the carcasses in a plastic bag in the freezer until you have three or four, then make stock. It may not have quite as rich a flavor as stock made from a whole bird or fresh wings, backs and necks, but it will still taste fresher and less salty than stock made from a cube.

5 When cold, remove the layer of fat that will have set on the surface.

STOCK TIPS

If wished, use a whole bird for making stock instead of wings, backs and necks. A stewing chicken will give wonderful flavor and provide plenty of chicken meat to use in soups and casseroles.

No salt is added to stock because as the stock reduces the flavor becomes concentrated and saltiness increases. Add salt to the dish in which the stock is used.

LIGHT LUNCHES

Meals in the middle of the day are often rushed affairs mid-week, so there are plenty of quick-to-prepare recipes here, such as Turkey Strips with Sour Cream Dip, or Thai Chicken and Vegetable Stir-fry. At the weekend, when there's more time to spare, try one of the marinated chicken dishes: Butterflied Cornish Game Hens are perfect if you are entertaining, while Minted Yogurt Chicken makes a delicious low fat family lunch.

Butterflied Cornish Game Hens

If you have time, do the preparation for this spicy dish the day before. The hens need to marinate for at least two hours, but if you leave them overnight the flavor will be even better.

INGREDIENTS

Serves 4
1 tbsp dry mustard powder
1 tbsp paprika
1 tbsp ground cumin
4 tsp tomato catsup
1 tbsp lemon juice
5 tbsp butter, melted
4 Cornish game hens, about 1lb each
salt

1 Mix together the mustard, paprika, ground cumin, catsup, lemon juice and salt until smooth, then gradually stir in the butter.

2 Using game shears or strong kitchen scissors, split each bird along one side of the backbone, then cut down the other side of the backbone to remove it.

3 Open out a hen, skin side uppermost, then press down firmly with the heel of your hand. Pass a long skewer through one leg and out through the other to secure the bird open and flat. Repeat the process with the remaining birds.

4 Spread the mustard mixture evenly over the skin of the birds. Cover loosely and leave in a cool place for at least 2 hours. Preheat a broiler.

5 Place the birds, skin side uppermost, under the broiler and cook for about 12 minutes. Turn the birds over, baste with any juices in the pan, and cook for a further 7 minutes, until the juices run clear.

COOK'S TIP

These hens cook very well on the barbecue, make sure the coals are very hot, then cook for 15–20 minutes, turning and basting frequently.

Cajun Chicken Jambalaya

INGREDIENTS

Serves 4

2½lb fresh chicken
1½ onions
1 bay leaf
4 black peppercorns
1 parsley sprig
2 tbsp vegetable oil
2 garlic cloves, chopped
1 green bell pepper, seeded and
 chopped
1 celery stalk, chopped
1¼ cups long grain rice
1 cup Chorizo sausage, sliced
1 cup chopped cooked ham
14oz can chopped tomatoes with herbs
½ tsp hot chili powder
½ tsp cumin seeds
½ tsp ground cumin
1 tsp dried thyme
1 cup cooked, peeled shrimp
dash of Tabasco sauce
chopped parsley, to garnish

1 Place the chicken in a large flame-proof casserole and pour over 2½ cups water. Add the half onion, the bay leaf, peppercorns and parsley and bring to a boil. Cover and simmer gently for about 1½ hours.

2 When the chicken is cooked lift it out of the stock, remove the skin and carcass and chop the meat. Strain the stock, leave to cool and reserve.

3 Chop the remaining onion and heat the oil in a large frying pan. Add the onion, garlic, green pepper and celery. Fry for about 5 minutes, then stir in the rice coating the grains with the oil. Add the sausage, ham and reserved chopped chicken and fry for a further 2–3 minutes, stirring frequently.

4 Pour in the tomatoes and 1¼ cups of the reserved stock and add the chili, cumin and thyme. Bring to a boil, then cover and simmer gently for 20 minutes, or until the rice is tender and the liquid absorbed.

5 Stir in the shrimp and Tabasco. Cook for a further 5 minutes, then season well and serve hot, garnished with chopped parsley.

Turkey Strips with Sour Cream Dip

INGREDIENTS

Serves 4

12oz turkey fillets, or 2 boneless
 breast portions
1 cup fine fresh bread crumbs
¼ tsp paprika
1 egg, lightly beaten
3 tbsp sour cream
1 tbsp ready-made tomato sauce
1 tbsp mayonnaise
salt and black pepper

1 Preheat the oven to 375°F. Cut the turkey into strips. Mix the bread crumbs with paprika and season with salt and pepper.

2 Dip the turkey into the egg, then into the bread crumbs, until thoroughly and evenly coated. Place on a baking sheet.

3 Cook the turkey in the top of the oven for 20 minutes, until crisp and golden. Turn once during cooking.

4 To make the dip, mix the sour cream, tomato sauce and mayonnaise together in a small bowl and season to taste. Serve the turkey strips with baked potatoes and a green salad or crisp green vegetables, accompanied by the dip.

Chicken, Bacon and Corn Kabobs

Don't wait for barbecue weather to have kabobs. If you are serving them to children, remember to remove the kabob sticks first.

INGREDIENTS

Serves 4

2 ears of corn, cooked
8 thick rashers bacon
8 brown cap mushrooms, halved
2 small chicken fillets
2 tbsp sunflower oil
1 tbsp lemon juice
1 tbsp maple syrup
salt and black pepper

1 Cook the corn in boiling water until tender, then drain and cool. Stretch the bacon rashers with the back of a knife; cut each in half. Wrap a piece around each half mushroom.

2 Cut both the corn and chicken into eight equal pieces. Mix together the oil, lemon juice, syrup and seasoning and brush liberally over the chicken.

3 Thread the corn, bacon-wrapped mushrooms and chicken pieces alternately on skewers and brush all over with the lemon dressing.

4 Broil the kabobs for 8–10 minutes, turning them once and basting occasionally with any extra dressing. Serve hot with either a crisp green or mixed leaf salad.

Turkey Pastitsio

A traditional Greek pastitsio is a rich, high-fat dish made with ground beef, but this lighter version is just as tasty.

INGREDIENTS 🍎

Serves 4–6
1lb lean ground turkey
1 large onion, finely chopped
4 tbsp tomato paste
1 cup red wine or stock
1 tsp ground cinnamon
2½ cups macaroni
1¼ cups skim milk
2 tbsp sunflower margarine
3 tbsp flour
1 tsp ground nutmeg
2 tomatoes, sliced
4 tbsp whole-wheat bread crumbs
salt and black pepper
green salad, to serve

1 Preheat the oven to 425°F. Cook the turkey and chopped onion in a nonstick pan without fat, stirring until lightly browned.

2 Stir in the tomato paste, red wine or stock, and cinnamon. Season, then cover and simmer for 5 minutes.

3 Cook the macaroni in boiling, salted water until just tender, then drain. Layer with the meat mixture in a wide ovenproof dish.

4 Place the milk, margarine, and flour in a saucepan and whisk over a moderate heat until thickened and smooth. Add the nutmeg, and salt and pepper to taste.

5 Pour the sauce evenly over the pasta and meat. Arrange the tomato slices on top and sprinkle lines of bread crumbs over the surface.

6 Bake for 30–35 minutes, or until golden brown and bubbling. Serve hot, with a green salad.

COOK'S TIP

If you can't find ground turkey, use ground chicken instead. And, if you are not too worried about the fat content then try this dish with ground lamb or beef.

Chicken with Herbs and Lentils

If your family doesn't like lentils (and some children don't) use rice instead.

INGREDIENTS

Serves 4

4oz piece of thick bacon or pork belly, rind removed, chopped
1 large onion, sliced
1¼ cups well-flavored chicken stock
bay leaf
2 sprigs each parsley, marjoram and thyme
2 cups green or brown lentils
4 chicken portions
salt and black pepper
2–4 tbsp garlic butter

1 Fry the bacon gently in a large, heavy-based flameproof casserole until all the fat runs out and the bacon begins to brown. Add the onions and fry for another 2 minutes.

2 Stir in the stock, bay leaf, herb stalks and some of the leafy parts (keep some herb sprigs for garnish), lentils and seasoning. Preheat the oven to 375°F.

3 Fry the chicken portions in a frying pan to brown the skin before placing on top of the lentils. Sprinkle with seasoning and some of the herbs.

4 Cover the casserole and cook in the oven for about 40 minutes. Serve with a tablespoon of garlic butter on each portion and a few of the remaining herb sprigs scattered over.

COOK'S TIP

For economy buy a smallish chicken and cut it in quarters, to give you four good-sized portions.

Chili-Chicken Couscous

Couscous is a very easy alternative to rice and makes a good base for all kinds of ingredients.

INGREDIENTS 🍎

Serves 4

2 cups couscous
4 cups boiling water
1 tsp olive oil
14oz chicken without skin and bone, diced
1 yellow bell pepper, seeded and sliced
2 large zucchini, sliced thickly
1 small green chili, thinly sliced, or 1 tsp chili sauce
1 large tomato, diced
15oz can chick-peas, drained
salt and black pepper
coriander or parsley sprigs, to garnish

1 Place couscous in a large bowl and pour over boiling water. Cover and let stand for 30 minutes.

2 Heat the oil in a large, non-stick pan and stir-fry the chicken quickly to seal, then reduce the heat.

3 Stir in the pepper, zucchini, and chili or sauce and cook for 10 minutes, until the vegetables are softened.

4 Stir in the tomato and chick-peas, then add the couscous. Adjust the seasoning and stir over moderate heat until hot. Serve garnished with sprigs of fresh coriander or parsley.

VARIATION

There's no need to stick exactly to the recipe, you could use whatever vegetables you have to hand – try small squashes, fine green beans, peas or fava beans in place of the zucchini.

Turkey and Bean Bake

INGREDIENTS 🍎

Serves 4

1 medium eggplant, thinly sliced
1 tbsp olive oil, for brushing
1lb turkey breast, diced
1 medium onion, chopped
14oz can chopped tomatoes
15oz can red kidney beans, drained
1 tbsp paprika
1 tbsp fresh chopped thyme, or 1 tsp dried
1 tsp chili sauce
1½ cups plain yogurt
½ tsp ground nutmeg
salt and black pepper

1 Preheat the oven to 375°F. Arrange the eggplant in a colander and sprinkle with salt.

2 Leave the eggplant for 30 minutes, then rinse and pat dry. Brush a non-stick pan with oil and cook the eggplant in batches, turning once, until golden.

3 Remove the eggplant, add the turkey and onion to the pan, then cook until lightly browned. Stir in the tomatoes, beans, paprika, thyme, chili sauce, and salt and pepper. In a separate bowl, mix together the yogurt and ground nutmeg.

4 Layer the meat and eggplant in an ovenproof dish, finishing with eggplant. Spread over the yogurt and bake for 50–60 minutes, until golden.

COOK'S TIP

Make sure that you dry the eggplant slices very thoroughly before frying. Squeeze them between sheets of paper towel – the drier the eggplant is, the less oil it will absorb.

Chinese-style Chicken Salad

INGREDIENTS

Serves 4
4 boneless chicken breasts (about 6oz each)
4 tbsp dark soy sauce
pinch of Chinese five spice powder
good squeeze of lemon juice
½ cucumber, peeled and cut into matchsticks
1 tsp salt
3 tbsp sunflower oil
2 tbsp sesame oil
1 tbsp sesame seeds
2 tbsp dry sherry
2 carrots, cut into matchsticks
8 scallions, shredded
1 cup beansprouts

For the sauce
4 tbsp chunky peanut butter
2 tsp lemon juice
2 tsp sesame oil
¼ tsp hot chili powder
1 scallion, finely chopped

1 Put the chicken portions into a large pan and just cover with water. Add 1 tbsp of the soy sauce, the Chinese five spice powder and lemon juice, cover and bring to a boil, then simmer for about 20 minutes.

2 Meanwhile, place the cucumber matchsticks in a colander, sprinkle with the salt and cover with a plate with a weight on top. Leave to drain for 30 minutes – set the colander in a bowl or on a deep plate to catch the drips.

3 Lift out the poached chicken with a slotted spoon and leave until cool enough to handle. Remove and discard the skins and pound the chicken lightly with a rolling pin to loosen the fibers. Slice into thin strips and reserve.

4 Heat the oils in a large frying pan or wok. Add the sesame seeds, fry for 30 seconds and then stir in the remaining 3 tbsp soy sauce and the sherry. Add the carrots and stir-fry for 2–3 minutes, until just tender. Remove from the heat and reserve.

5 Rinse the cucumber well, pat dry with paper towel and place in a bowl. Add the scallions, beansprouts, cooked carrots, pan juices and shredded chicken, and mix together. Transfer to a shallow dish. Cover and chill for about 1 hour, turning the mixture in the juices once or twice.

6 To make the sauce, cream the peanut butter with the lemon juice, sesame oil and chili powder, adding a little hot water to form a paste, then stir in the scallion. Arrange the chicken mixture on a serving dish and serve with the peanut sauce.

Stir-fried Turkey with Snow Peas

INGREDIENTS

Serves 4

2 tbsp sesame oil
6 tbsp lemon juice
1 garlic clove, crushed
½in piece fresh ginger root, peeled
  and grated
1 tsp honey
1lb turkey fillets, cut into strips
4oz snow peas, trimmed
2 tbsp groundnut oil
⅓ cup cashew nuts
6 scallions, cut into strips
8oz can water chestnuts, drained and
  thinly sliced
salt
saffron rice, to serve

1 Mix together the sesame oil, lemon juice, garlic, ginger and honey in a shallow non-metallic dish. Add the turkey and mix well. Cover and leave to marinate for 3–4 hours.

2 Blanch the snow peas in boiling salted water for 1 minute. Drain and refresh under cold running water.

3 Drain the marinade from the turkey strips and reserve the marinade. Heat the groundnut oil in a wok or large frying pan, add the cashew nuts and stir-fry for about 1–2 minutes until golden brown. Remove the cashew nuts from the wok or frying pan using a slotted spoon and set aside.

4 Add the turkey and stir-fry for 3–4 minutes, until golden brown. Add the scallions, snow peas, water chestnuts and the reserved marinade. Cook for a few minutes, until the turkey is tender and the sauce is bubbling and hot. Stir in the cashew nuts

Italian Chicken

INGREDIENTS

Serves 4

2 tbsp flour
4 chicken pieces (legs, breasts
  or quarters)
2 tbsp olive oil
1 onion, chopped
2 garlic cloves, chopped
1 red bell pepper, seeded
  and chopped
14oz can chopped tomatoes,
2 tbsp ready-made pesto sauce
4 sun-dried tomatoes in oil,
  chopped
⅔ cup chicken stock
1 tsp dried oregano
8 black olives, pitted
salt and black pepper
chopped fresh basil and basil leaves,
  to garnish
tagliatelle, to serve

1 Place the flour and seasoning in a paper bag. Add the chicken pieces and shake well until coated. Heat the oil in a flameproof casserole, add the chicken and brown quickly. Remove the chicken and set aside.

2 Lower the heat, add the onion, garlic and pepper and cook for 5 minutes. Stir in the other ingredients, except the olives, and bring to a boil.

3 Return the sautéed chicken pieces to the casserole, season lightly, cover and simmer for 30–35 minutes, or until the chicken is cooked.

4 Add the olives and simmer for a further 5 minutes. Transfer to a warmed serving dish, sprinkle with the chopped basil and garnish with basil leaves. Serve with hot tagliatelle.

Honey and Orange Glazed Chicken

This way of cooking chicken breasts is popular in America, Australia and Great Britain. It is ideal for an easy evening meal served with baked potatoes.

INGREDIENTS

Serves 4

4 x 6oz boneless chicken breasts
1 tbsp oil
4 scallions, chopped
1 garlic clove, crushed
3 tbsp honey
4 tbsp fresh orange juice
1 orange, peeled and segmented
2 tbsp soy sauce
fresh lemon balm or flat leaf parsley,
  to garnish
baked potatoes and mixed salad,
  to serve

1 Preheat the oven to 375°F. Place the chicken breasts in a shallow roasting pan and set aside.

2 Heat the oil in a small pan, and fry the scallions and garlic for about 2 minutes until softened. Add the honey, orange juice, orange segments and soy sauce to the pan, stirring well until the honey has dissolved.

3 Pour over the chicken and bake, uncovered, for about 45 minutes, basting once or twice until the chicken is cooked. Garnish with lemon balm or parsley and serve the chicken and its sauce with baked potatoes and a salad.

— COOK'S TIP —

Look out for mustard flavored with honey to add to this dish instead of the honey.

Thai Chicken and Vegetable Stir-fry

INGREDIENTS

Serves 4

1 piece lemon grass (or the rind of
  ½ lemon)
½in piece of fresh ginger root
1 large garlic clove, chopped
2 tbsp sunflower oil
10oz lean chicken, thinly sliced
½ red pepper, seeded and sliced
½ green pepper, seeded and sliced
4 scallions, chopped
2 medium carrots, cut into matchsticks
4oz fine green beans
2 tbsp oyster sauce
pinch sugar
salt and black pepper
¼ cup salted peanuts, lightly crushed,
and coriander leaves, to garnish

1 Thinly slice the lemon grass or lemon rind. Peel and chop the ginger and garlic. Heat the oil in a frying pan over a high heat until hazy. Add the lemon grass or lemon rind, ginger and garlic, and stir-fry for 30 seconds until brown.

2 Add the chicken and stir-fry for 2 minutes. Then add the vegetables and stir-fry for 4–5 minutes, until the chicken is cooked and the vegetables are almost cooked.

3 Finally stir in the oyster sauce, sugar and seasoning to taste and stir-fry for another minute to mix and blend well. Serve the stir-fry at once, sprinkled with the peanuts and coriander leaves and accompanied by rice.

COOK'S TIP

Make this quick supper dish a little hotter by adding more fresh ginger root, if you wish.

Pasta with Turkey and Tomatoes

INGREDIENTS

Serves 4

1½lb ripe but firm plum
  tomatoes, quartered
6 tbsp olive oil
1 tsp dried oregano
12oz broccoli florets
1 small onion, sliced
1 tsp dried thyme
1lb turkey breast fillets, cubed
3 garlic cloves, finely chopped
1 tbsp fresh lemon juice
12oz dried pasta twists
salt and black pepper

1 Preheat the oven to 400°F. Place the tomatoes in a baking dish. Drizzle over 1 tbsp of the oil, scatter over the oregano and season with salt.

2 Bake for 30–40 minutes, until the tomatoes are just browned.

3 Meanwhile, bring a large pan of salted water to the boil. Add the broccoli and cook for about 5 minutes, until just tender. Drain the broccoli and set aside. Alternatively, steam the broccoli until tender.

-------- COOK'S TIP --------

Plum tomatoes are perfect for this dish, but if they are unavailable use any well-flavored, firm, yet ripe variety – even tiny cherry tomatoes.

4 Heat 2 tbsp of the remaining oil in a large non-stick frying pan. Add the onion, thyme, turkey and salt, to taste. Cook over a high heat for 5–7 minutes, stirring frequently, until the meat is cooked and beginning to brown. Add the garlic and cook for a further 1 minute, stirring frequently.

5 Remove from the heat. Stir in the lemon juice and season with pepper. Set aside and keep warm.

6 Bring another large pan of salted water to the boil. Add the pasta and cook for 10–12 minutes, until just tender. Drain and place in a large serving bowl. Toss the pasta with the remaining oil.

7 Add the broccoli to the turkey mixture and toss into the pasta. Peel the tomatoes and stir gently into the pasta mixture. Serve immediately.

Chicken with Honey and Grapefruit

Chicken breast portions cook very quickly and are ideal for suppers 'on-the-run' - but don't be tempted to overcook them. You could substitute boneless turkey steaks, or duck breast fillets for the chicken, if you like.

INGREDIENTS

Serves 4
4 chicken breast portions, skinned
3–4 tbsp honey
1 pink grapefruit, peeled and cut into
   12 segments
salt and black pepper
three-colored noodles and salad leaves,
   to serve

1 Make three quite deep, diagonal slits in the chicken flesh using a large sharp knife.

2 Brush the chicken with honey, and season. Preheat broiler.

3 Place the chicken in a flameproof dish, uncut side uppermost, under a medium broiler for 2–3 minutes, then turn over and place the grapefruit segments in the slits. Brush with more honey and cook for 5 minutes, or until tender.

4 If necessary, reduce the heat so that the honey glazed parts don't burn. Serve at once with three-coloured noodles and salad leaves.

Crispy Chicken with Garlicky Rice

Chicken wings cooked until they are really tender have a surprising amount of meat on them, and make a very economical supper for a crowd of youngsters – provide lots of kitchen paper or napkins for the sticky fingers.

INGREDIENTS

Serves 4
1 large onion, chopped
2 garlic cloves, crushed
2 tbsp sunflower oil
$^7/_8$ cup patna or basmati rice
1½ cups hot chicken stock
2 tsp finely grated lemon rind
2 tbsp chopped mixed herbs
8 or 12 chicken wings
½ cup flour
salt and black pepper

1 Preheat the oven to 400°F. Fry the onion and garlic in the oil in a large ovenproof pan until golden. Add the patna or basmati rice and toss until well coated in oil.

2 Stir in the stock, lemon rind and herbs and bring to a boil. Cover and cook in the middle of the oven for 40–50 minutes. Stir the rice once or twice during cooking.

3 Meanwhile, wipe dry the chicken wings. Season the flour and use to coat the chicken portions thoroughly, dusting off any excess.

4 Place the chicken wings in a small roasting pan and cook in the top of the oven for 30–40 minutes, turning once, until crispy and golden.

5 Serve the rice and the crispy chicken wings together with a fresh tomato sauce and a selection of vegetables.

Turkey Spirals

These little spirals may look difficult, but they're very simple to make, and a very good way to pep up plain turkey.

INGREDIENTS

Serves 4

4 thinly sliced turkey breasts, about 3½oz each
4 tsp tomato paste
½ cup large basil leaves
1 garlic clove, crushed
1 tbsp skim milk
2 tbsp whole-wheat flour
salt and black pepper
fresh tomato sauce and pasta with fresh basil, to serve

1 Place the turkey steaks on a board. If too thick, flatten them slightly by beating with a rolling pin.

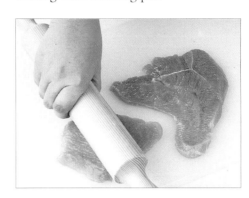

2 Spread each turkey breast with tomato paste, then top with a few leaves of basil, a little crushed garlic, and salt and pepper.

3 Roll up firmly around the filling and secure with a toothpick. Brush with milk and sprinkle with flour to coat lightly.

4 Place the spirals on a foil-lined broiler pan. Cook under a broiler for 15–20 minutes, turning them occasionally, until thoroughly cooked. Serve hot, sliced with a spoonful or two of fresh tomato sauce and pasta, sprinkled with fresh basil.

COOK'S TIP

When flattening the turkey breasts with a rolling pin, place them between two sheets of plastic wrap. Tap them gently and evenly so the meat thins, but doesn't break.

Caribbean Chicken Kabobs

These kabobs have a rich, sunshine Caribbean flavor and the marinade keeps them moist without the need for oil. Serve with a colorful salad and rice.

INGREDIENTS

Serves 4
1¼lb boneless chicken breasts, skinned
finely grated rind of 1 lime
2 tbsp lime juice
1 tbsp rum or sherry
1 tbsp brown sugar
1 tsp ground cinnamon
2 mangoes, peeled and cubed
rice and salad, to serve

1 Cut the chicken into bite-sized chunks and place in a bowl with the lime rind and juice, rum, sugar, and cinnamon. Toss well, cover, and leave to marinate for 1 hour.

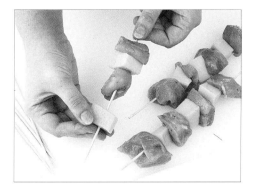

2 Save the juices and thread the chicken onto four wooden skewers, alternating with the mango cubes.

3 Cook the skewers under a broiler, or on a barbecue, for about 8–10 minutes, turning occasionally and basting with the juices, until the chicken is tender and golden brown. Serve at once, with rice and salad.

——— COOK'S TIP ———

The rum or sherry adds a lovely rich flavor to the marinade, but it is optional so can be omitted if you prefer to avoid the added alcohol

---

——— VARIATION ———

Try other fruits in place of the mangoes – chunks of fresh pineapple or firm peaches or nectarines would be equally good in this recipe.

Chicken with White Wine and Olives

INGREDIENTS

Serves 4

3½lb chicken, cut into pieces
1 onion, sliced
3–6 garlic cloves, finely chopped
1 tbsp dried thyme
2 cups dry white wine
16–18 pitted green olives
1 bay leaf
1–2 tbsp butter
black pepper
fresh bay leaves and lemon rind,
   to garnish

1 Heat a large, heavy frying pan. when hot, add the chicken pieces, skin-side down, and cook over a medium heat for about 10 minutes, until browned. Turn over the chicken pieces and brown the other side for about 5–8 minutes more.

2 Tranfer the chicken to a platter and set aside.

3 Drain the excess fat from the pan, leaving about 1 tbsp. Add the sliced onion and ½ tsp salt and cook for about 5 minutes, until just soft. Add the garlic and thyme and cook for a further 1 minute.

4 Add the wine and stir, scraping up any bits that cling to the pan. Bring to the boil and boil for about 1 minute, then stir in the green olives.

5 Return the chicken pieces to the pan. Add the bay leaf and season lightly with pepper. Reduce the heat, cover and simmer for 20–30 minutes, until the chicken is cooked through.

6 Transfer the chicken pieces to a warm serving dish. Stir the lemon juice into the sauce and whisk in the butter to thicken the sauce slightly. Spoon the sauce over the chickenm and serve at once, garnished with bay leaves and lemon rind.

Turkey Meat Loaf

INGREDIENTS

Serves 4

1 tbsp olive oil
1 onion, chopped
1 green bell pepper, seeded and finely
   chopped
1 garlic cloves, finely chopped
1lb ground turkey
1 cup fresh white bread crumbs
1 egg, beaten
½ cup pine nuts
12 sun-dried tomatoes in oil, drained
   and chopped
⅓ cup milk
1 bay leaf
2 tsp chopped fresh rosemary or
   ½ tsp dried
1 tsp fennel seeds
½ tsp dried oregano
salt and black pepper

1 Preheat the oven to 375°F. Heat the oil in a frying pan. Add the onion, green pepper and galic and cook over a low heat for 8–10 minutes, stirring frequently, until the vegetables are just softened. Remove from the heat and leave to cool.

2 Place the minced turkey in a large bowl. Add the onion mixture and all the remaining ingredients and mix together thoroughly.

3 Transfer to a 8 x 4½in loaf pan, packing down firmly. Bake for about 1 hour, until golden brown. Serve with a salad.

Mandarin Sesame Duck

Duck is a high-fat meat but it is possible to get rid of a good proportion of the fat cooked in this way. (If you remove the skin completely, the meat can be dry.) For a special occasion, duck breasts are a good choice, but they are more expensive.

INGREDIENTS 🍎

Serves 4

4 duck legs or boneless breasts
2 tbsp light soy sauce
3 tbsp clear honey
1 tbsp sesame seeds
4 mandarin oranges
1 tsp cornflour
salt and black pepper

1 Preheat the oven to 350°F. Prick the duck skin all over. Slash the breast skin diagonally at intervals with a sharp knife.

2 Place the duck on a rack in a roasting pan and roast for 1 hour. Mix 1 tbsp soy sauce with 2 tbsp honey and brush over the duck. Sprinkle with sesame seeds. Roast for 15–20 minutes, until golden brown.

3 Meanwhile, grate the rind from one mandarin and squeeze the juice from two. Mix in the cornstarch, then stir in the remaining soy sauce and honey. Heat, stirring, until thickened and clear. Season. Peel and slice the remaining mandarins. Serve the duck, with the mandarin slices and the sauce.

---- COOK'S TIP ----

Use tangerines or clementines, or 1–2 large oranges in place of the mandarins, if you prefer.

Minted Yogurt Chicken

INGREDIENTS 🍎

Serves 4

8 chicken thighs, skinned
1 tbsp clear honey
2 tbsp lime or lemon juice
2 tbsp natural yogurt
4 tbsp chopped fresh mint
salt and black pepper

1 Slash the chicken flesh at intervals with a sharp knife. Place in a bowl.

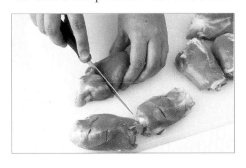

2 Mix the honey, lime or lemon juice, yogurt, seasoning and half the mint.

3 Spoon the marinade over the chicken and leave to marinate for 30 minutes. Line a grill pan with foil and cook the chicken under a broiler until thoroughly cooked and golden brown, turning the chicken occasionally during cooking.

4 Sprinkle with the remaining chopped mint. Serve with potatoes and tomato salad.

---- VARIATION ----

To make Herby Yogurt Chicken substitute 60ml/4 tbsp mixed chopped herbs, such as parsley, thyme and chives.

Oven-fried Chicken

INGREDIENTS

Serves 4
4 large chicken portions
½ cup plain flour
½ tsp salt
¼ tsp black pepper
1 egg
2 tbsp water
2 tbsp finely chopped mixed fresh
  herbs, such as parsley, basil, and
  thyme
1 cup dried white bread crumbs
¼ cup freshly grated Parmesan cheese
lemon wedges, to serve

2 Combine the flour, salt and pepper on a large plate and stir with a fork to mix. Coat the chicken portions on all sides with the seasoned flour and shake off the excess.

1 Preheat the oven to 400°F. Rinse the chicken portions and pat dry with kitchen paper.

3 Sprinkle a little water on to the chicken portions and coat again lightly with the seasoned flour.

4 Beat the egg with the water in a shalow dish and stir in the herbs. Dip the chicken portions into the egg mixture, turning to coat them evenly.

5 Combine the bread crumbs and grated Parmesan cheese on a plate. Roll the chicken portions in the bread cumbs, patting them in with your finger tips to help them stick.

6 Place the chicken portions in a greased shallow pan large enough to hold them in one layer. Bake for 20–30 minutes, until thoroughly cooked and golden brown. To test whether they are cooked, prick with a fork: the juices that run out should be clear, not pink. Serve at once with lemon wedges.

Chicken in Creamy Orange Sauce

This sauce is deceptively creamy – in fact it is made with low fat ricotta, which is virtually fat-free. The brandy adds a richer flavor, but is optional – omit it if you prefer and use orange juice alone.

INGREDIENTS

Serves 4

8 chicken thighs or drumsticks, skinned
3 tbsp brandy
1¼ cups orange juice
3 scallions, chopped
2 tsp cornstarch
6 tbsp low fat ricotta
salt and black pepper

1 Cook the chicken pieces without fat in a non-stick or heavy pan, turning until evenly browned.

2 Stir in the brandy, orange juice and scallions. Bring to a boil, then cover and simmer for 15 minutes, or until the chicken is tender and the juices run clear, not pink, when pierced.

3 Blend the cornstarch with a little water then mix into the ricotta. Stir this into the sauce and stir over moderate heat until boiling.

4 Adjust the seasoning and serve with boiled rice or pasta and green salad.

————— COOK'S TIP —————

Cornstarch stabilizes the ricotta cheese and helps prevent it curdling.

————— VARIATION —————

To make Turkey in Creamy Orange Sauce, substitute 4 turkey steaks for the chicken tighs or drumsticks.

Chicken with Lemon and Herbs

The herbs can be changed according to what is available; for example, parsley or thyme could be used instead of tarragon and fennel.

INGREDIENTS

Serves 2

4 tbsp butter
2 scallions, white part only, finely chopped
1 tbsp chopped fresh tarragon
1 tbsp chopped fresh fennel
juice of 1 lemon
4 chicken thighs
salt and black pepper
lemon slices and herb sprigs, to garnish

1 Preheat the broiler to moderate. In a small saucepan, melt the butter, then add the scallions, herbs, lemon juice and seasoning.

2 Brush the chicken thighs generously with the herb mixture, then broil for 10–12 minutes, basting frequently with the herb mixture.

3 Turn over the chicken and baste again, then cook for a further 10–12 minutes or until the chicken juices run clear.

4 Serve the chicken garnished with lemon slices and herb sprigs, and accompanied by any remaining herb mixture.

Chicken with Red Cabbage

INGREDIENTS

Serves 4

4 tbsp butter
4 large chicken portions, halved
1 onion, chopped
1¼lb red cabbage, finely shredded
4 juniper berries, crushed
12 cooked chestnuts
½ cup full-bodied red wine
salt and black pepper

2 Add the onion to the casserole and fry gently until soft and light golden brown. Stir the cabbage and juniper berries into the casserole, season and cook over a moderate heat for 6–7 minutes, stirring once or twice.

1 Heat the butter in a heavy flame-proof casserole and lightly brown the chicken pieces. Transfer to a plate.

3 Stir the chestnuts into the casserole, then tuck the chicken pieces under the cabbage so they are on the bottom of the casserole. Pour in the red wine.

4 Cover and cook gently for about 40 minutes until the chicken juices run clear and the cabbage is very tender. Check the seasoning and serve.

Tandoori Chicken Kabobs

This dish originates from the plains of the Punjab at the foot of the Himalayas. There food is traditionally cooked in clay ovens known as *tandoors* – hence the name.

INGREDIENTS

Serves 4
4 boneless, skinless chicken breasts
    (about 6oz each)
1 tbsp lemon juice
3 tbsp tandoori paste
3 tbsp natural yogurt
1 garlic clove, crushed
2 tbsp chopped fresh coriander
1 small onion, cut into wedges and
    separated into layers
a little oil, for brushing
salt and black pepper
fresh coriander sprigs, to garnish
pilau rice and naan bread, to serve

1 Chop the chicken breasts into 1in cubes, place in a bowl and add the lemon juice, tandoori paste, yogurt, garlic, coriander and seasoning. Cover and leave to marinate in the fridge for 2–3 hours.

2 Preheat the broiler. Thread alternate pieces of marinated chicken and onion on to four skewers.

3 Brush the onions with a little oil, lay on a broiling rack and cook under a high heat for 10–12 minutes, turning once. Garnish the kebabs with fresh coriander and serve at once with pilau rice and naan bread.

> — COOK'S TIP —
>
> Use chopped, boned and skinless chicken thighs, or turkey breasts for a cheaper alternative.

Chinese Chicken with Cashew Nuts

INGREDIENTS

Serves 4
4 boneless, skinless chicken breasts
    (about 6oz each), and into thin
    strips
3 garlic cloves, crushed
4 tbsp soy sauce
2 tbsp cornflour
8oz dried egg noodles
3 tbsp groundnut or sunflower oil
1 tbsp sesame oil
1 cup roasted cashew nuts
6 spring onions, cut into 5cm/2in
    pieces and halved lengthways
spring onion curls and a little chopped
    red chilli, to garnish

1 Place the chicken in a bowl with the garlic, soy sauce and cornflour and mix until the chicken is well coated. Cover and chill for about 30 minutes.

2 Meanwhile, bring a pan of water to the boil and add the egg noodles. Turn off the heat and leave to stand for 5 minutes. Drain well and reserve.

3 Heat the oils in a large frying pan or wok and add the chilled chicken and marinade juices. Stir-fry on a high heat for about 3–4 minutes, or until golden brown.

4 Add the cashew nuts and spring onions to the pan or wok and stir-fry for 2–3 minutes.

5 Add the drained noodles and stir-fry for a further 2 minutes. Toss the noodles well and serve immediately, garnished with the spring onion curls and chopped chilli.

New Hampshire Farmhouse Flan

INGREDIENTS

Serves 4

2 cups whole wheat flour
4 tbsp butter, cubed
4 tbsp lard
1 tsp caraway seeds
1 tbsp oil
1 onion, chopped
1 garlic clove, crushed
2 cups chopped cooked chicken
2½ cups washed and chopped
  watercress leaves
grated rind of ½ small lemon
2 eggs, lightly beaten
¾ cup heavy cream
3 tbsp natural yogurt
good pinch of grated nutmeg
3 tbsp grated Cheddar cheese
beaten egg, to glaze
salt and black pepper

1 Place the flour in a bowl with a pinch of salt. Add the butter and lard and rub into the flour with your fingertips until the mixture resembles bread crumbs. (Alternatively, you can use a food processor.)

2 Stir in the caraway seeds and 3 tbsp iced water and mix thoroughly to make a firm dough. Knead lightly on a floured surface until smooth.

3 Roll out the pastry on a lightly floured surface and use to line a 7 x 11in loose-based pie pan. Reserve the pastry trimmings. Prick the base and chill for 20 minutes. Place a baking sheet in the oven and preheat to 400°F.

4 Heat the oil in a frying pan and sauté the onion and garlic for 5–6 minutes, until just softened. Remove from the heat and cool.

5 Line the pastry shell with waxed paper and fill with baking beans. Bake for 10 minutes, then remove the paper and beans and cook for a further 5 minutes.

6 Mix together the onion, chicken, watercress and lemon rind and spoon into the tart shell. Beat the eggs, cream, yogurt, nutmeg, cheese and seasoning and pour over the chicken mix.

7 Roll out the pastry trimmings and cut out ½in strips. Brush with egg, then twist each strip and lay in a lattice over the tart. Press the ends on to the pastry edge. Bake for 35 minutes, until the top is golden. Serve warm or cold.

Chicken Biryani

INGREDIENTS

Serves 4

1½ cups basmati rice, rinsed
½ tsp salt
5 whole cardamom pods
2–3 whole cloves
1 cinnamon stick
3 tbsp vegetable oil
3 onions, sliced
1½lb boneless, skinless chicken
   (4 x 6oz chicken breasts), cubed
¼ tsp ground cloves
5 cardamom pods, seeds removed
   and ground
¼ tsp hot chili powder
1 tsp ground cumin
1 tsp ground coriander
½ tsp freshly ground black pepper
3 garlic cloves, finely chopped
1 tsp finely chopped fresh ginger root
juice of 1 lemon
4 tomatoes, sliced
2 tbsp chopped fresh coriander
⅔ cup natural yogurt
½ tsp saffron strands soaked in 2 tsp
   hot milk
3 tbsp toasted flaked almonds and fresh
   coriander sprigs, to garnish
natural yogurt, to serve

1 Preheat the oven to 375°F. Bring a pan of water to a boil and add the rice, salt, ground cardamom, cloves and cinnamon stick. Boil for 2 minutes and then drain, leaving the whole spices in the rice.

2 Heat the oil in a pan and fry the onions for about 8 minutes, until browned. Add the chicken followed by all the ground spices, the garlic, ginger and lemon juice. Stir-fry for 5 minutes.

3 Transfer the chicken mixture to an ovenproof casserole and lay the tomatoes on top. Sprinkle over the fresh coriander, spoon over the yogurt and top with the drained rice.

4 Drizzle the saffron and milk mixture over the rice and then pour over about ⅔ cup water.

5 Cover tightly and bake in the oven for 1 hour. Transfer to a warmed serving platter and remove the whole spices from the rice. Garnish with toasted almonds and fresh coriander and serve with yogurt.

DINNER PARTY DISHES

Chicken, duck, turkey and game dishes are ideal if you are
entertaining – not too expensive, generally light to eat and, on the
whole, quick and easy to prepare. There are dishes here suitable
for special occasions and celebrations, such as Venison with
Cranberry Sauce, or Turkey with Yellow Pepper Sauce, and
other simpler, yet equally delicious recipes for unexpected
guests – try Duck Breasts with Orange.

Normandy Roast Chicken

INGREDIENTS

Serves 4

4 tbsp butter, softened
2 tbsp chopped fresh tarragon
1 small garlic clove, crushed
3lb fresh chicken
1 tsp flour
⅔ cup light cream or crème fraîche
good squeeze of lemon juice
salt and black pepper
fresh tarragon and lemon slices,
    to garnish

1 Preheat the oven to 400°F. Mix together the butter, 1 tbsp of the chopped tarragon, the garlic and seasoning in a bowl. Spoon half the butter into the cavity of the chicken.

2 Carefully lift the skin at the neck end of the bird away from the breast flesh on each side, then gently push a little of the butter into each pocket and smooth down over the breast with your fingers.

3 Season the bird and lay it, breast down, in a roasting pan. Roast in the oven for 45 minutes, then turn the chicken over and baste with the juices. Cook for a further 45 minutes.

4 When the chicken is cooked, lift it to drain out any juices from the cavity into the pan, then transfer the bird to a warmed platter.

5 Place the roasting pan on the burner and heat until sizzling. Stir in the flour and cook for 1 minute, then stir in the cream, the remaining tarragon, ⅔ cup water, the lemon juice and seasoning. Boil and stir for 2–3 minutes, until thickened. Garnish the chicken with tarragon and lemon slices and serve with the sauce.

Duck Breasts with Orange Sauce

A simple variation on the classic French whole roast duck.

INGREDIENTS

Serves 4

4 duck breasts
1 tbsp sunflower oil
2 oranges
⅔ cup fresh orange juice
1 tbsp port
2 tbsp Seville orange marmalade
1 tbsp butter
1 tsp cornstarch
salt and black pepper

1 Season the duck breast skin. Heat the oil in a frying pan over a moderate heat and add the duck breasts, skin side down. Cover and cook for 3–4 minutes, until lightly browned. Turn the breasts over, lower the heat slightly and cook uncovered for 5–6 minutes.

2 Peel the skin and pith from the oranges. Working over a bowl to catch any juice, slice either side of the membranes to release the orange segments, then set aside with the juice.

3 Remove the duck breasts from the pan with a slotted spoon, drain on paper towel and keep warm in the oven while making the sauce. Drain off the fat from the pan.

4 Add the segmented oranges, all but 2 tbsp of the orange juice, the port and the orange marmalade to the pan. Bring to a boil and then reduce the heat slightly. Whisk small dabs of the butter into the sauce and season.

5 Blend the cornstarch with the reserved orange juice, pour into the pan and stir until slightly thickened. Add the duck breasts and cook gently for about 3 minutes. To serve, arrange the sliced breasts on plates with the sauce.

Venison with Cranberry Sauce

Venison steaks are now readily available. Lean and low in fat, they make a healthy choice for a special occasion. Served with a sauce of fresh seasonal cranberries, port and ginger, they make a dish with a wonderful combination of flavors.

INGREDIENTS

Serves 4

1 orange
1 lemon
1 cup fresh or frozen cranberries, picked over
1 tsp grated fresh ginger root
1 thyme sprig
1 tsp Dijon mustard
4 tbsp red currant jelly
²⁄₃ cup ruby port
2 tbsp sunflower oil
4 venison steaks
2 shallots, finely chopped
salt and black pepper
thyme sprigs, to garnish
creamy mashed potatoes and broccoli, to serve

1 Pare the rind from half the orange and half the lemon using a vegetable peeler, then cut the rind into very fine strips.

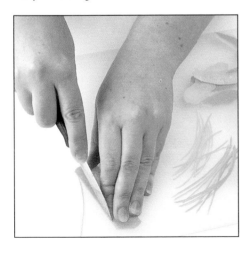

2 Blanch the strips in a small pan of boiling water for about 5 minutes until tender. Drain the strips and refresh under cold water.

3 Squeeze the juice from the orange and lemon and then pour into a small pan. Add the fresh or frozen cranberries, ginger, thyme sprig, mustard, red currant jelly and port. Cook over a low heat until the jelly melts.

4 Bring the sauce to a boil, stirring occasionally, then cover the pan and reduce the heat. Cook gently, for about 15 minutes, until the cranberries are just tender.

5 Heat the oil in a heavy-based frying pan, add the venison steaks and cook over a high heat for 2–3 minutes.

6 Turn over the steaks and add the shallots to the pan. Cook the steaks on the other side for 2–3 minutes, depending on whether you like rare or medium cooked meat.

7 Just before the end of cooking, pour in the sauce and add the strips of orange and lemon rind.

8 Leave the sauce to bubble for a few seconds to thicken slightly, then remove the thyme sprig and adjust the seasoning to taste.

9 Transfer the venison steaks to warmed plates and spoon over the sauce. Garnish with thyme sprigs and serve accompanied by creamy mashed potatoes and broccoli.

COOK'S TIP

When frying venison, always remember the briefer the better; venison will turn to leather if subjected to fierce heat after it has reached the medium-rare stage. If you dislike any hint of pink, cook it to this stage then let it rest in a low oven for a few minutes.

VARIATION

When fresh cranberries are unavailable, use red currants instead. Stir them into the sauce towards the end of cooking with the orange and lemon rinds.

Rabbit with Parsley Sauce

INGREDIENTS

Serves 4
6 tbsp soy sauce
few drops of Tabasco sauce
1 tbsp sweet paprika
1 tbsp dried basil
2–3lb rabbit, cut into pieces
3 tbsp peanut or olive oil
¾ cup flour
1 large onion, finely sliced
1 cup dry white wine
1 cup chicken stock
2 cloves garlic, finely chopped
4 tbsp fresh chopped parsley
salt and white pepper
mashed potatoes or rice, to serve
fresh parsley sprigs, to garnish

1 Combine the soy sauce, Tabasco sauce, white pepper, paprika, and basil in a medium-sized bowl. Add the rabbit pieces and turn them over in the mixture so they are coated thoroughly. Let marinate at least 1 hour.

2 Heat the oil in a flameproof casserole. Coat the rabbit pieces lightly in the flour, shaking off the excess. Brown the rabbit pieces in the hot oil for about 5–6 minutes, turning them frequently. Remove the rabbit pieces with a slotted spoon and set aside on a plate or dish. Preheat the oven to 350°F.

3 Add the onion to the casserole and cook over a low heat for 8–10 minutes, until softened. Increase the heat, add the wine, and stir well to mix in all the cooking juices.

4 Return the rabbit and any juices to the casserole. Add the stock, garlic, parsley and salt. Mix well and turn the rabbit to coat with the sauce. Cover and place in the oven. Cook for about 1 hour, until the rabbit is tender, stirring occasionally. Serve garnished with parsley sprig and accompanied by mashed potatoes or rice.

Cajun-spiced Chicken

INGREDIENTS

Serves 6

6 medium skinless boneless chicken
  breasts
6 tbsp butter or margarine
1 tsp garlic powder
2 tsp onion powder
2 tsp cayenne pepper
2 tsp paprika
1½ tsp salt
½ tsp white pepper
1 tsp black pepper
¼ tsp ground cumin
1 tsp dried thyme
salad leaves and bell pepper strips,
  to garnish

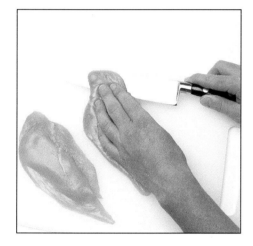

1 Slice each chicken breast in half horizontally, making two pieces of about the same thickness. Flatten them slightly with the heel of your hand.

2 Melt the butter or margarine in a small saucepan over a low heat.

VARIATION

For Cajun-spiced Fish substitute six white fish fillets for the chicken. Do not slice the fish fillets in half, but season as for the chicken and cook for 2 minutes on one side and 1½–2 minutes on the other, until the fish flakes easily.

3 Combine all the remaining ingredients in a bowl and stir to blend well. Brush the chicken pieces on both sides with a little of the melted butter or margarine, then sprinkle evenly with the seasoning mixture.

4 Heat a large heavy-based frying pan over high heat for about 5–8 minutes, until a drop of water sprinkled on the surface sizzles.

5 Drizzle 1 tsp melted butter on to each chicken piece. Place them in the frying pan in an even layer, two or three at a time, and cook for 2–3 minutes, until the underside begins to blacken. Turn and cook the other side for 2–3 minutes more. Serve hot with salad leaves and pepper strips.

Lemon Chicken with Guacamole Sauce

INGREDIENTS

Serves 4

juice of 2 lemons
3 tbsp olive oil
2 garlic cloves, finely chopped
4 chicken breasts, about 7oz each
2 large tomatoes, cored and cut in half
chopped fresh coriander, to garnish
salt and black pepper

For the sauce

1 ripe avocado
4 tbsp sour cream
3 tbsp fresh lemon juice
½ tsp salt
¼ cup water

1 Combine the lemon juice, oil, garlic, ½ tsp salt and a little pepepr in a bowl. Stir to mix.

VARIATION

To barbecue the chicken, prepare the fire, and when the coals are glowing red and covered with grey ash, spread them in a single layer. Set an oiled rack about 5in above the coals and cook the chicken breasts for about 15–20 minutes until lightly charred and cooked through, brushing with oil, to baste.

2 Arrange the chicken breasts, in one layer, in a shallow glass or ceramic dish. Pour over the lemon mixture and turn to coat evenly. Cover and leave to stand for at least 1 hour at room temperature, or chill overnight.

3 To make the sauce, halve the avocado, remove the stone and scrap the flesh into a food processor.

4 Add the sour cream, lemon juice and salt and process until smooth. Add the water and process just to blend. If necessary, add a little more water to thin the sauce. Transfer to a bowl, taste and adjust the seasoning if necessary. Set aside in a cool place.

5 Preheat the broiler and heat a ridged frying pan. Remove the chicken from the marinade and pat dry.

6 When the frying pan is hot, add the chicken breasts and cook for about 10 minutes, turning them frequently, until they are cooked through.

7 Meanwhile, arrange the tomato halves, cut-sides up, on a baking sheet and season lightly with salt and black pepper. Broil for about 5 minutes, until hot and bubbling.

8 To serve, place a chicken breast, tomato half and a dollop of avocado sauce on each plate. Sprinkle with chopped coriander and serve.

Pheasant with Apples

Pheasant is worth buying as it is low in fat, full of flavour, and never dry when cooked like this.

INGREDIENTS

Serves 4
1 pheasant
2 small onions, quartered
3 celery stalks, thickly sliced
2 red eating apples, thickly sliced
½ cup stock
1 tbsp clear honey
2 tbsp Worcestershire sauce
ground nutmeg
2 tbsp toasted hazelnuts
salt and black pepper

1 Preheat the oven to 350°F. Sauté the pheasant without fat in a non-stick pan, turning occasionally until golden. Remove and keep hot.

2 Sauté the onions and celery in the pan to brown lightly. Spoon into a casserole and place the pheasant on top. Tuck the apple slices around it.

3 Spoon over the stock, honey, and Worcestershire sauce. Sprinkle with nutmeg, salt and pepper, cover, and bake for 1¼ –1½ hours or until tender. Sprinkle with nuts and serve hot.

——————— VARIATION ———————

Choose a firm variety of eating apple for this recipe, less acidic fruits hold their shape best.

Cider-baked Rabbit

Rabbit is a low fat meat and an economical choice for family meals.

INGREDIENTS

Serves 4
1lb rabbit pieces
1 tbsp flour
1 tsp dry mustard
3 medium leeks, thickly sliced
1 cup dry cider
2 sprigs rosemary
salt and black pepper
fresh rosemary, to garnish

1 Preheat the oven to 350°F. Place the rabbit pieces in a bowl and sprinkle over the flour and mustard. Toss to coat evenly.

2 Arrange the rabbit in one layer in a wide casserole. Blanch the leeks in boiling water, then drain and add to the casserole.

3 Add the cider, rosemary, and seasoning, cover, then bake for 1–1¼ hours, or until the rabbit is tender. Garnish with fresh rosemary, and serve with baked potatoes and vegetables.

——————— VARIATION ———————

To make Cider-baked Chicken, substitute small chicken joints, such as thighs or drumsticks for the rabbit pieces.

Oat-coated Chicken with Sage

Rolled oats make a good coating for savory foods, and offer a good way to add extra fiber.

INGREDIENTS 🍎

Serves 4
3 tbsp skim milk
2 tsp plain mustard
½ cup rolled oats
3 tbsp chopped sage leaves
8 chicken thighs or drumsticks, skinned
½ cup low fat cream cheese
1 tsp whole-grain mustard
salt and black pepper
fresh sage leaves, to garnish

1 Preheat the oven to 400°F, then mix together the milk and plain mustard until smooth.

2 Mix the oats with 2 tbsp of the sage and the seasoning on a plate. Brush the chicken with the milk and press into the oats to coat.

3 Place the chicken on a baking sheet and bake for about 40 minutes, or until the juices run clear, not pink, when pierced through the thickest part.

4 Meanwhile, mix together the low fat cream cheese, mustard, remaining sage and seasoning, then serve with the chicken. Garnish the chicken with fresh sage and serve hot or cold.

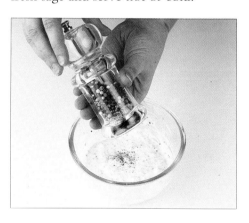

---- COOK'S TIP ----

If fresh sage is not available, choose another fresh herb such as thyme or parsley, instead of using a dried alternative.

---- VARIATION ----

For the sauce, use natural yogurt or Italian ricotta cheese in place of the cream cheese, if you prefer.

Turkey with Yellow Pepper Sauce

INGREDIENTS

Serves 4

2 tbsp olive oil
2 large yellow bell peppers, seeded
  and chopped
1 small onion, chopped
1 tbsp freshly squeezed orange
  juice
1¼ cups chicken stock
4 turkey escalopes
3oz Boursin or garlicky cream
  cheese
12 fresh basil leaves
2 tbsp butter
salt and black pepper

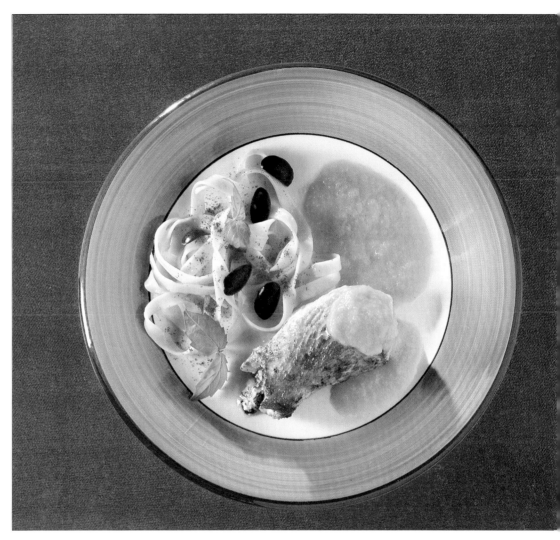

1 To make the yellow pepper sauce; heat half the oil in a pan and gently fry the peppers and onion until beginning to soften. Add the orange juice and stock and cook until very soft.

2 Meanwhile, lay the turkey escalopes out flat and pound them out lightly.

3 Spread the turkey escalopes with the Boursin or garlicky cream cheese. Chop half the basil and sprinkle on top, then roll up, tucking in the ends like an envelope, and secure neatly with half a toothpick.

4 Heat the remaining oil and the butter in a frying pan and fry the escalopes for 7–8 minutes, turning them frequently, until golden and cooked.

5 While the escalopes are cooking, press the pepper mixture through a sieve, or blend until smooth, then strain back into the pan. Season to taste and warm through, or serve cold, with the escalopes, garnished with the remaining basil leaves.

COOK'S TIP

Chicken breast fillets or veal escalopes could be used in place of the turkey, if you prefer.

Crumbed Turkey Steaks

The authentic Austrian recipe for *Weiner Schnitzel* uses veal escalopes (in fact the recipe originated from Milan in Italy, where Parmesan cheese replaced the bread crumbs.) Turkey breasts make a good alternative.

INGREDIENTS

Serves 4
4 turkey breast steaks (about 5oz each)
3 tbsp flour, seasoned
1 egg, lightly beaten
1½ cups fresh bread crumbs
5 tbsp finely grated Parmesan cheese
2 tbsp butter
3 tbsp sunflower oil
fresh parsley, to garnish
4 lemon wedges, to serve

1 Lay the turkey steaks between two sheets of waxed paper. Pound each one with a rolling pin until flattened. Snip the edges of the steaks with scissors a few times to prevent them curling during cooking.

2 Place the seasoned flour on one plate, the egg into another and the bread crumbs and Parmesan mixed together on a third plate.

3 Dip each side of the steaks into the flour and shake off any excess. Next, dip them into the egg and then gently press each side into the bread crumbs and cheese until evenly coated.

4 Heat the butter and oil in a large frying pan and fry the turkey steaks on a moderate heat for 2–3 minutes on each side, until golden. Garnish with parsley and serve with lemon wedges.

Country Cider Hot-pot

Game casseroles are popular all over the British Isles.

INGREDIENTS

Serves 4
2 tbsp flour
4 boneless rabbit pieces
2 tbsp butter
1 tbsp vegetable oil
15 baby onions
4 strips lean bacon, chopped
2 tsp Dijon mustard
1⅞ cups apple cider
3 carrots, chopped
2 parsnips, chopped
12 ready-to-eat prunes, pitted
1 fresh rosemary sprig
1 bay leaf
salt and black pepper

1 Preheat the oven to 325°F. Place the flour and seasoning in a plastic bag, add the rabbit pieces and shake until coated. Set aside.

2 Heat the butter and oil in a flame-proof casserole and add the onions and bacon. Fry for 4 minutes, until the onions have softened. Remove with a draining spoon and reserve.

3 Fry the seasoned rabbit pieces in the oil in the flameproof casserole until they are browned all over, then spread a little of the mustard over the top of each piece.

4 Return the onions and bacon to the pan. Pour on the cider and add the carrots, parsnips, prunes, rosemary and bay leaf. Season well. Bring to a boil, then cover and transfer to the oven. Cook for about 1½ hours until tender.

5 Remove the rosemary sprig and bay leaf and serve the rabbit hot with creamy mashed potatoes.

Chicken, Pepper and Bean Stew

INGREDIENTS

Serves 4
4lb chicken, cut into pieces
paprika
2 tbsp olive oil
2 tbsp butter
2 onions, chopped
½ each green and yellow bell pepper,
   chopped
2 cups peeled, chopped, fresh or
   canned plum tomatoes
1 cup white wine
2 cups chicken stock
   or water
3 tbsp chopped fresh parsley
½ tbsp Tabasco sauce
1 tbsp Worcestershire sauce
2 x 7oz can corn kernels
4oz fava beans (fresh or frozen)
3 tbsp flour
salt and black pepper
fresh parsley sprigs, to garnish

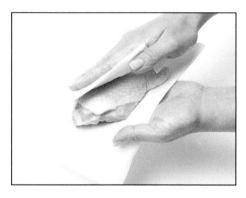

1 Rinse the chicken pieces under cold water and pat dry with kitchen paper. Sprinkle each piece lightly with salt and a little paprika.

2 Heat the olive oil with the butter in a flame proof casserole or large heavy-based saucepan over a medium-high heat, until the mixture is sizzling and just starting to change color.

3 Add the chicken pieces and fry until golden brown on all sides, cooking in batches, if necessary. Remove from the pan with tongs and set aside

4 Reduce the heat and add the onions and peppers to the pan. Cook for 8–10 minutes, until softened.

5 Increase the heat. Add the tomatoes and their juice, the wine, stock or water, parsley and Tabasco sauce and Worcestershire sauce. Stir thoroughly and bring to the boil.

6 Add the chicken to the pan, pushing down into the sauce. Cover, reduce the heat, and simmer for 30 minutes, stirring occasionally.

7 Remove the lid, add the corn and beans and mix well. Partly cover the pan and cook for 30 minutes.

8 Tilt the pan and skim off as much of the surface fat as possible. Mix the flour with a little water in a small bowl to make a paste.

9 Stir in about ¾ cup of the hot sauce from the pan into the flour mixture and then stir into the stew and mix well. Cook for 5–8 minutes more, stirring occasionally.

10 Check the seasoning and adjust if necessary. Serve the stew in shallow soup dishes or large bowls, garnished with parsley sprigs.

Cornish Game Hens in Vermouth

INGREDIENTS

Serves 4

4 Cornish game hens, about
  1lb each
4 tbsp butter, softened
2 shallots, chopped
4 tbsp chopped fresh parsley
8oz white grapes, preferably
  muscatel, halved and seeded
⅔ cup white vermouth
1 tsp cornstarch
4 tbsp heavy cream
2 tbsp pine nuts, toasted
salt and black pepper
watercress sprigs, to garnish

1 Preheat the oven to 400°F. Wash and dry the Cornish hens. Spread the softened butter all over the birds and put a hazelnut-sized piece in the cavity of each.

2 Mix together the shallots and parsley and place a quarter of the mixture inside each bird. Put them side by side in a large roasting pan and roast for 40–50 minutes, or until the juices run clear when the thickest part of the flesh is pierced with a skewer. Transfer the Cornish hens to a warmed serving plate. Cover and keep warm.

3 Skim off most of the fat from the roasting pan, then add the grapes and vermouth. Place the pan directly over a low flame for a few minutes to warm and slightly soften the grapes.

4 Lift the grapes out of the pan using a slotted spoon and scatter them around the birds. Keep covered. Stir the cornstarch into the cream, then add to the pan juices. Cook gently for a few minutes, stirring, until the sauce has thickened. Taste and adjust seasoning.

5 Pour the sauce around the Cornish hens. Sprinkle with the toasted pine nuts and garnish with watercress sprigs.

Guinea Hen with Cider and Apples

Guinea hens are farmed, so they are available quite frequently in super-markets, usually fresh. Their flavor is reminiscent of an old-fashioned chicken – not really gamey, but they do have slightly darker meat.

INGREDIENTS

Serves 4–6
4–4½lb guinea hen
1 onion, halved
3 celery stalks
3 bay leaves
little butter
1¼ cups dry cider
⅔ cup chicken stock
2 small apples, peeled and sliced
4 tbsp thick heavy cream
few sage leaves
2 tbsp chopped fresh parsley
salt and black pepper

1 If the guinea hen is packed with its giblets, put them in a pan with water to cover, half the onion, a stalk of celery, a bay leaf and seasoning. Simmer for 30 minutes, or until you have about ⅔ cup well-flavored stock.

2 Preheat the oven to 375°F. Wash and wipe dry the bird and place the remaining onion half and a table-spoon of butter inside the body cavity. Place in a roasting dish, sprinkle with seasoning to taste, and dot with a few tablespoons of butter.

3 Pour the cider and chicken stock into the dish and cover with a lid or foil. Bake for 25 minutes per 1 lb, basting occasionally.

4 Uncover for the last 20 minutes, baste well again and add the pre-pared apples and the celery, sliced. When the guinea hen is cooked, trans-fer it to a warm serving dish and keep warm. Remove the apples and celery with a slotted spoon and set aside.

5 Boil the liquid rapidly to reduce to about ⅔ cup. Stir in the cream, seasoning to taste and the sage leaves, and cook for a few minutes more to reduce slightly. Return the apples to this pan with the parsley and warm through, then serve with or around the bird.

Coronation Chicken

INGREDIENTS

Serves 8

½ lemon
5lb chicken
1 onion, quartered
1 carrot, quartered
large bouquet garni
8 black peppercorns, crushed
salt
watercress sprigs, to garnish

For the sauce

1 small onion, chopped
1 tbsp butter
1 tbsp curry paste
1 tbsp tomato paste
½ cup red wine
bay leaf
juice of ½ lemon, or more to taste
2–3 tsp apricot preserve
1¼ cups mayonnaise
½ cup whipping cream, whipped
salt and black pepper

1 Put the lemon half in the chicken cavity, then place the chicken in a saucepan that it just fits. Add the vegetables, bouquet garni, peppercorns and salt to the pan.

2 Add sufficient water to come two-thirds of the way up the chicken, bring to the boil, then cover and cook gently for about 1½ hours, until the chicken juices run clear.

3 Transfer the chicken to a large bowl, pour over the cooking liquid and leave to cool. When cold, skin and bone the chicken, then chop.

4 Make the sauce, cook the onion in the butter until soft. Add the curry paste, tomato paste, wine, bay leaf and lemon juice, then cook for 10 minutes. Add the jam, then sieve and cool.

5 Beat into the mayonnaise. Fold in the cream, then add seasoning and lemon juice, then stir in the chicken.

Duck with Cumberland Sauce

INGREDIENTS

Serves 4

4 duck portions
grated rind and juice of 1 lemon
grated rind and juice of 1 large orange
4 tbsp red currant jelly
4 tbsp port
pinch of ground mace or ginger
1 tbsp brandy
salt and black pepper
orange slices, to garnish

2 Meanwhile, simmer the lemon and orange juices and rinds together in a saucepan for 5 minutes.

1 Preheat the oven to 375°F. Place a rack in a roasting pan. Prick the duck portions all over, sprinkle with salt and pepper. Place the duck portions on the rack and cook in the oven for 45–50 minutes, until the duck skin is crisp and the juices run clear.

3 Stir in the red currant jelly until melted, then stir in the port. Bring to the boil, add mace or ginger and seasoning to taste.

4 Transfer the duck to a serving plate; keep warm. Pour the fat from the roasting pan, leaving the cooking juices. With the pan over a low heat, stir in the brandy, dislodging the sediment and bring to the boil. Stir in the port sauce and serve with the duck, garnished with orange slices.

Chicken in Green Sauce

Slow, gentle cooking makes the chicken succulent and tender.

INGREDIENTS

Serves 4
2 tbsp butter
1 tbsp olive oil
4 chicken portions
1 small onion, finely chopped
⅔ cup medium-bodied dry white wine
⅔ cup chicken stock
6oz watercress
2 thyme sprigs and 2 tarragon sprigs
⅔ cup heavy cream
salt and black pepper
watercress leaves, to garnish

1 Heat the butter and oil in a heavy shallow pan, then brown the chicken evenly. Transfer the chicken to a plate using a slotted spoon and keep warm in the oven.

2 Add the onion to the cooking juices in the pan and cook until softened but not coloured.

3 Stir in the wine, boil for 2–3 minutes, then add the stock and bring to the boil. Return the chicken to the pan, cover tightly and cook very gently for about 30 minutes, until the chicken juices run clear. Then transfer the chicken to a warm dish, cover the dish and keep warm.

4 Boil the cooking juices hard until reduced to about 4 tbsp. Remove the leaves from the watercress and herbs, add to the pan with the cream and simmer over a medium heat until slightly thickened.

5 Return the chicken to the casserole, season and heat through for a few minutes. Garnish with watercress leaves to serve.

COOK'S TIP

You could use boneless turkey steaks in place of the chicken portions in this recipe, if you prefer.

Tuscan Chicken

This simple peasant casserole has all the flavors of traditional Tuscan ingredients. The wine can be replaced by chicken stock.

INGREDIENTS

Serves 4

8 chicken thighs, skinned
1 tsp olive oil
1 medium onion, sliced thinly
2 red bell peppers, seeded and sliced
1 garlic clove, crushed
1¼ cups puréed tomatoes
⅔ cup dry white wine
large sprig fresh oregano, or 1 tsp dried oregano
14oz can cannellini beans, drained
3 tbsp fresh bread crumbs
salt and black pepper

1 Cook the chicken in the oil in a non-stick or heavy pan until golden brown. Remove and keep hot. Add the onion and bell peppers to the pan and gently sauté until softened, but not brown. Stir in the garlic.

2 Add the chicken, tomatoes, wine, and oregano. Season well, bring to a boil, then cover the pan tightly.

COOK'S TIP

In the summer, when fresh herbs are abundant, stir in a handful of fresh chopped parsley just before sprinkling with the bread crumbs.

3 Lower the heat and simmer gently, stirring occasionally for 30–35 minutes or until the chicken is tender and the juices run clear, not pink, when pierced with the point of a knife.

4 Stir in the cannellini beans and simmer for 5 minutes more, until heated through. Sprinkle with the bread crumbs and cook under a broiler until golden brown.

Duck Breasts with Blackberries

If there isn't any blackberry, or bramble, jelly in your kitchen cupboard, you could substitute red currant jelly instead.

INGREDIENTS

Serves 4
4 duck breasts
finely grated rind and juice of 1 orange
2 tbsp blackberry (bramble) jelly
salt and black pepper

1 Heat a heavy-based frying pan and place the duck portions skin side down first. Fry for 3–4 minutes. Meanwhile, sprinkle the meat side with seasoning and the orange rind.

2 Turn the duck over and continue cooking for 3–4 minutes. Spread the skin side with some of the blackberry jelly while cooking, and pour the orange juice over the portions.

3 Spread a little more jelly over the duck breasts, then turn them over and cook for 1–2 minutes more, until just cooked, but still slightly pink in the middle. Serve the duck breasts with the glaze poured over, accompanied by new potatoes and a watercress and orange salad.

Spring Rabbit Casserole

If you have never tried rabbit before, you will find it very similar to chicken, but with just a slightly sweeter taste. You could replace the rabbit with chicken in this recipe, if you prefer – cook it in exactly the same way.

INGREDIENTS

Serves 4
1 tbsp sunflower oil
1lb boneless rabbit
4 rashers bacon, rinded and chopped
2 leeks, sliced
4 scallions, sliced
3 celery stalks, chopped
4 small carrots, sliced
1¼ cups vegetable stock
2 tsp Dijon mustard
1 tsp grated lemon rind
3–4 tbsp crème fraîche or sour cream
salt and black pepper
herby mashed potatoes, to serve

1 Heat the oil in a large flameproof casserole and fry the rabbit pieces until browned all over. Preheat the oven to 375°F.

2 Add the bacon and vegetables and toss over the heat for 1 minute. Add the stock, mustard, lemon rind and crème fraîche or sour cream, and seasoning to taste, then bring to the boil.

3 Cover and cook for 35–40 minutes, or until the rabbit is tender (it should take no longer than chicken). Serve with herby mashed potatoes – creamed potatoes well flavored and colored with chopped fresh parsley and snipped chives.

ROASTS, PIES & HOT-POTS

Slow-cooked casseroles have a wonderful flavor: try the delicious
Pheasant with Mushrooms, or an easy-to-prepare Turkey
Hot-pot. If you would prefer a roast, make a delicious stuffing for
chicken with celery root, or prepare it Italian-style with a colorful
tomato coat. Pies are perfect weekend fare, and there are plenty
here to choose from. Try Curried Chicken and Apricot Pie on
your family, or enclose chicken fillets and herby butter in flaky
filo to make delightful individual pastry parcels.

Farmhouse Venison Pie

A simple and satisfying pie – venison in a rich gravy, topped with potato and parsnip mash.

Ingredients

Serves 4
3 tbsp sunflower oil
1 onion, chopped
1 garlic clove, crushed
3 rashers lean bacon, chopped
1½lb ground venison
4oz button mushrooms, chopped
2 tbsp flour
1⅞ cups beef stock
⅔ cup ruby port
2 bay leaves
1 tsp chopped fresh thyme
1 tsp Dijon mustard
1 tbsp red currant jelly
1½lb potatoes
1lb parsnips
1 egg yolk
4 tbsp butter
freshly grated nutmeg
3 tbsp chopped fresh parsley
salt and black pepper

1 Heat the oil in a large frying pan and fry the onion, garlic and bacon for about 5 minutes. Add the venison and mushrooms and cook for a few minutes, stirring, until browned.

2 Stir in the flour and cook for 1–2 minutes, then add the stock, port, herbs, mustard, red currant jelly and seasoning. Bring to a boil, cover and simmer for 30–40 minutes, until tender. Spoon into a large pie dish or four individual ovenproof dishes.

3 While the venison and mushroom mixture is cooking, preheat the oven to 400°F. Cut the potatoes and parsnips into large chunks. Cook together in boiling salted water for 20 minutes or until tender. Drain and mash, then beat in the egg yolk, butter, nutmeg, chopped parsley and seasoning.

4 Spread the potato and parsnip mixture over the meat and bake for 30–40 minutes, until piping hot and golden brown. Serve at once.

Chicken and Ham Pie

This domed double-crust pie is suitable for a cold buffet, for picnics or any packed meals.

INGREDIENTS

Serves 8

14oz ready-made shortcrust pie
  pastry
1¾lb chicken breast
12oz uncooked ham
about 4 tbsp heavy cream
6 scallions, finely chopped
1 tbsp chopped fresh tarragon
2 tsp chopped fresh thyme
grated rind and juice of ½ large
  lemon
1 tsp grated nutmeg
salt and black pepper
beaten egg or milk, to glaze

1 Preheat the oven to 190°F. Roll out one-third of the pastry and use it to line a 8in pie pan 2in deep. Place the pie pan on a cookie sheet. Set aside.

2 Grind 4oz of the chicken with the ham, then mix with the cream, scallions, herbs, lemon rind, 1tbsp of the lemon juice and the seasoning to make a soft mixture; add a little more heavy cream if necessary.

3 Cut the remaining chicken into ½in pieces and mix with the remaining lemon juice, the grated nutmeg and seasoning to taste.

4 Make a layer of one-third of the ham mixture in the pie shell, cover with half the chopped chicken, then add another layer of one-third of the ham mixture. Add all the remaining chicken followed by the remaining ham.

5 Dampen the edges of the pie shell. Roll out the remaining pastry to make a lid for the pie.

6 Use the trimmings to make a lattice decoration. Make a small hole in the center of the pie, brush the top with beaten egg or milk, then bake for about 20 minutes. Reduce the oven temperature to 325°F and bake for a further 1–1¼ hours; cover the top with foil if the pastry becomes too brown. Transfer the pie to a wire rack and leave to cool.

Chicken, Leek and Parsley Pie

INGREDIENTS

Serves 4–6

For the pastry
2½ cups flour
pinch of salt
⅞ cup butter, diced
2 egg yolks

For the filling
3 part-boned chicken breasts
flavoring ingredients (bouquet garni,
   black peppercorns, onion and carrot)
4 tbsp butter
2 leeks, thinly sliced
2oz Cheddar cheese, grated
1oz Parmesan cheese, finely grated
3 tbsp chopped fresh parsley
2 tbsp whole grain mustard
1 tsp cornstarch
1¼ cups heavy cream
salt and black pepper
beaten egg, to glaze
mixed green salad, to serve

1 To make the pastry, first sift the
flour and salt. Blend together the
butter and egg yolks in a food processor until creamy. Add the flour and
process until the mixture is just coming
together. Add about 1 tbsp cold water
and process for a few seconds more.
Turn out on to a lightly floured surface
and knead lightly. Wrap in plastic wrap
and chill for about 1 hour.

2 Meanwhile, poach the chicken
breasts in water to cover, with the
flavoring ingredients added, until
tender. Leave to cool in the liquid.

3 Preheat the oven to 400°F. Divide
the pastry into two pieces, one
slightly larger than the other. Roll out
the larger piece on a lightly floured
surface and use to line a 7 x 11in
baking dish or pan. Prick the base
with a fork and bake for 15 minutes.
Leave to cool.

4 Lift the cooled chicken from the
poaching liquid and discard the
skins and bones. Cut the chicken flesh
into strips, then set aside.

5 Melt the butter in a frying pan and
fry the leeks over a low heat,
stirring occasionally, until soft.

6 Stir in the Cheddar, Parmesan and
chopped parsley. Spread half the
leek mixture over the cooked pastry
base, leaving a border all the way
around. Cover the leek mixture with
the chicken strips, then top with the
remaining leek mixture.

7 Mix together the mustard, cornstarch
and cream in a small bowl. Add
seasoning to taste. Pour over the filling.

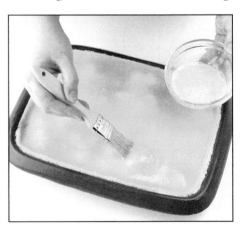

8 Moisten the edges of the cooked
pastry base. Roll out the remaining
pastry and use to cover the pie. Brush
with beaten egg and bake for 30–40
minutes until golden and crisp. Serve
hot, cut into square portions, with a
mixed green salad.

COOK'S TIP

This pastry is quite fragile and may break;
the high fat content, however, means you
can patch it together by pressing pieces of
pastry trimmings into any cracks.

Chicken Parcels with Herb Butter

INGREDIENTS

Serves 4

4 chicken breast fillets, skinned
10 tbsp butter, softened
6 tbsp chopped fresh mixed herbs,
  such as thyme, parsley, oregano
  and rosemary
1 tsp lemon juice
5 large sheets filo pastry, defrosted
  if frozen
1 egg, beaten
2 tbsp grated Parmesan cheese
salt and black pepper

1 Season the chicken fillets and fry in 2 tbsp of the butter to seal and brown lightly. Allow to cool.

2 Preheat the oven to 375°F. Put the remaining butter, the herbs, lemon juice and seasoning in a food processor and process until smooth. Melt half the herb butter.

3 Take one sheet of filo pastry and brush with herb butter. Fold the filo pastry sheet in half and brush again with butter. Place a chicken fillet about 1in from the top end.

4 Dot the chicken with a quarter of the remaining herb butter. Fold in the sides of the pastry, then roll up to enclose it completely. Place seam-side down on a lightly greased baking sheet. Repeat with the other chicken fillets.

5 Brush the filo parcels with beaten egg. Cut the last sheet of filo into strips, then scrunch and arrange on top. Brush the parcels once again with the egg glaze, then sprinkle with Parmesan. Bake for about 35–40 minutes, until golden brown. Serve hot.

Stoved Chicken

'Stoved' is derived from the French *étouffer* – to cook in a covered pot – and originates from the Franco/Scottish 'Alliance' of the seventeenth century.

INGREDIENTS

Serves 4
2lb potatoes, cut into ¼in slices
2 large onions, thinly sliced
1 tbsp chopped fresh thyme
2 tbsp butter
1 tbsp oil
2 large slices bacon, chopped
4 large chicken joints, halved
bay leaf
2½ cups chicken stock
salt and black pepper

1 Preheat the oven to 300°F. Make a thick layer of half the potato slices in the bottom of a large, heavy casserole, then cover with half the onion. Sprinkle with half the thyme, and seasonings.

--- COOK'S TIP ---

Instead of buying large chicken joints and cutting them in half, choose either chicken thighs or chicken drumsticks – or use a mixture of the two.

2 Heat the butter and oil in a large frying pan, then brown the bacon and chicken. Using a slotted spoon, transfer the chicken and bacon to the casserole. Reserve the fat in the pan.

3 Sprinkle the remaining thyme and some seasoning over the chicken, then cover with the remaining onion, followed by a neat layer of overlapping potato slices. Sprinkle with seasoning.

4 Pour the stock into the casserole, brush the potatoes with the reserved fat, then cover tightly and cook in the oven for about 2 hours, until the chicken is tender.

5 Preheat the broiler. Uncover the casserole and place under the broiler and cook until the slices of potato are beginning to brown and crisp. Serve the chicken hot.

Pot-roast of Venison

INGREDIENTS

Serves 4–5

4–4½lb boned joint of venison
5 tbsp oil
4 cloves
8 black peppercorns, lightly crushed
12 juniper berries, lightly crushed
1 cup full-bodied red wine
4oz lightly smoked bacon, chopped
2 onions, finely chopped
2 carrots, chopped
5oz large mushrooms, sliced
1 tbsp flour
1 cup veal stock
2 tbsp red currant jelly
salt and black pepper

1 Put the venison in a bowl, add half the oil, the spices and wine, cover and leave in a cool place for 24 hours, turning the meat occasionally.

2 Preheat the oven to 325°F. Remove the venison from the bowl and pat dry. Reserve the marinade. Heat the remaining oil in a shallow pan, then brown the venison evenly. Transfer to a plate.

3 Stir the bacon, onions, carrots and mushrooms into the pan and cook for about 5 minutes. Stir in the flour and cook for 2 minutes, then remove from the heat and stir in the marinade, stock, red currant jelly and seasoning. Return to the heat, bring to the boil, stirring, then simmer for 2–3 minutes.

4 Transfer the venison and sauce to a casserole, cover and cook in the oven, turning the joint occasionally, for about 3 hours, until tender.

Pheasant with Mushrooms

INGREDIENTS

Serves 4

1 pheasant, jointed
1 cup red wine
3 tbsp oil
4 tbsp Spanish sherry vinegar
1 large onion, chopped
2 slices smoked bacon, cut into strips
12oz brown mushrooms, sliced
3 anchovy fillets, soaked for 10 minutes and drained
1½ cups game, veal or chicken stock
bouquet garni
salt and black pepper

2 Preheat the oven to 325°F. Lift the pheasant from the dish, pat dry. Reserve the marinade.

3 Heat the remaining oil in a flame-proof casserole, then brown the pheasant joints. Transfer to a plate.

4 Add the bacon and remaining onion to the casserole and cook until the onion is soft. Stir in the mushrooms and cook for about 3 minutes.

5 Stir in the anchovies and remaining vinegar, boil until reduced. Add the marinade, cook for 2 minutes, then add the stock and bouquet garni. Return the pheasant to the casserole, cover and bake for about 1½ hours. Transfer the pheasant to a serving dish. Boil the cooking juices to reduce. Discard the bouquet garni. Pour over the pheasant and serve at once.

1 Place the pheasant in a dish, add the wine, half the oil and half the vinegar, and scatter over half the onion. Season, then cover and leave in a cool place for 8–12 hours, turning the pheasant occasionally.

Cornish Chicken Pie

This traditional dish comes from Cornwall in England and so cream is used in the filling.

INGREDIENTS

Serves 4
4 tbsp butter
4 chicken legs
1 onion, finely chopped
⅔ cup milk
⅔ cup sour cream
4 scallions, quartered
¾oz fresh parsley leaves, finely chopped
8oz ready-made puff pastry
½ cup heavy cream
2 eggs, beaten, plus extra for glazing
salt and black pepper

1 Melt the butter in a heavy-based, shallow pan, then brown the chicken legs. Transfer to a plate.

2 Add the chopped onion to the pan and cook until softened but not browned. Stir the milk, sour cream, scallions, parsley and seasoning into the pan, bring to the boil, then simmer for a couple of minutes stirring occasionally.

3 Return the chicken to the pan with any juices, then cover tightly and cook very gently over a low heat for about 30 minutes. Transfer the chicken and sauce mixture to a 5 cup pie dish and leave to cool.

4 Meanwhile, roll out the pastry until about ¾in larger all round than the top of the pie dish. Leave the pastry to relax while the chicken is cooling.

5 Preheat the oven to 425°F. Cut off a narrow strip around the edge of the pastry, then place the strip on the edge of the pie dish. Moisten the strip, then cover the dish with the pastry. Press the edges together.

6 Make a hole in the center of the pastry and insert a small funnel of foil. Brush the pastry with beaten egg, then bake for 15–20 minutes.

7 Reduce the oven temperature to 350°F. Mix the cream and eggs, then pour into the pie through the funnel. Shake the pie to distribute the cream, then return to the oven for 5–10 minutes. Remove the pie from the oven and leave in a warm place for 5–10 minutes before serving, or cool completely if serving cold.

Normandy Pheasant

Cider, apples and cream make this a rich and flavorful dish.

INGREDIENTS

Serves 4
2 oven-ready pheasants
1 tbsp olive oil
2 tbsp butter
4 tbsp Calvados or Apple Jack
1⅞ cups cider
bouquet garni
3 crisp eating apples, peeled, cored
  and thickly sliced
⅔ cup heavy cream
salt and black pepper
thyme sprigs, to garnish

1 Preheat the oven to 325°F. Joint both pheasants into four pieces using a large sharp knife. Discard the backbones and knuckles.

2 Heat the oil and butter in a large flameproof casserole. Working in two batches, add the pheasant pieces to the casserole and brown them over a high heat. Return all the pheasant pieces to the casserole.

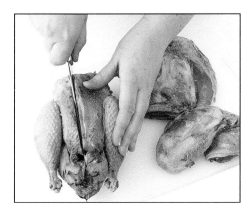

3 Standing well back, pour over the Calvados or apple jack and set it alight. When the flames have subsided, pour in the cider, then add the bouquet garni and seasoning and bring to a boil. Cover and cook for 50 minutes.

4 Tuck the apple slices around the pheasant. Cover and cook for 5–10 minutes, or until the pheasant is tender. Transfer the pheasant and apple to a warmed serving plate. Keep warm.

5 Remove the bouquet garni, then reduce the sauce by half to a syrupy consistency. Stir in the cream and simmer for a further 2–3 minutes until thickened. Taste the sauce and adjust the seasoning. Spoon the sauce over the pheasant and serve hot, garnished with thyme sprigs.

Chicken and Mushroom Pie

INGREDIENTS

Serves 6

½oz dried porcini mushrooms
4 tbsp butter
2 tbsp flour
1 cup hot chicken stock
¼ cup single cream or milk
1 onion, coarsely chopped
2 carrots, sliced
2 celery stalks, coarsely chopped
2oz fresh mushrooms, quartered
1lb cooked chicken meat, cubed
2oz fresh or frozen peas
salt and black pepper
beaten egg, to glaze

For the pastry

2 cups flour
¼ tsp salt
½ cup cold butter, cubed
⅓ cup white cooking fat, cubed
4–8 tbsp iced water

1 To make the pastry, sift the flour and salt into a bowl. With a pastry blender or two knives, cut in the butter and cooking fat until the mixture resembles bread crumbs. Sprinkle with 6 tbsp iced water and mix until the dough holds together. If the dough is too crumbly, add a little more water, 1 tbsp at a time. Gather the dough into a ball and flatten into a round. Place in a sealed polythene bag a chill for at least 30 minutes.

2 Place the porcini mushrooms in a small bowl. Add hot water to cover the mushrooms and leave to soak for about 30 minutes, until soft. Lift out of the water with a slotted spoon to leave any grit behind and drain on kitchen paper. Discard the soaking water. Preheat the oven to 375°F.

3 Melt half of the butter in a heavy-based saucepan. Whisk in the flour and cook until bubbling, whisking constantly. Add the warm stock and cook over a medium heat, whisking, until the mixture boils. Cook for 2–3 minutes more, then whisk in the cream or milk. Season with salt and pepper and set aside.

4 Heat the remaining butter in a large non-stick frying pan until sizzling. Add the onion and carrots and cook for about 5 minutes, until softenend. Add the celery and fresh mushrooms and cook for a further 5 minutes. Stir in the cooked chicken, peas and drained porcini mushrooms.

5 Add the chicken mixture to the cream sauce and stir to mix. Taste for seasoning. Turn into a 4 pint rectangular baking dish.

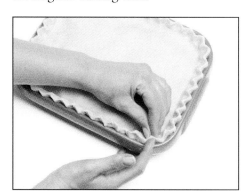

6 Roll out the dough to about a ⅛in thickness. Cut out a rectangle about 1in larger all around than the dish. Lay the rectangle of dough over the filling. Make a decorative edge by pushing the index finger of one hand between the thumb and index finger of the other.

7 Cut several slits in the pastry to allow steam to escape then brush the pastry with the beaten egg.

8 Press together the pastry trimmings and roll out again. Cut into thin strips and lay them over the pastry lid. Glaze again. If liked, roll small balls of dough and arrange them in the "windows" in the lattice.

9 Bake for about 30 minutes, until the pastry is browned. Serve the pie hot from the dish.

Mixed Game Pie

INGREDIENTS

Serves 4

1lb game meat, off the bone (plus the
  carcasses and bones)
1 small onion, halved
2 bay leaves
2 carrots, halved
few black peppercorns
1 tbsp oil
3oz bacon pieces, rinded and
  chopped
1 tbsp flour
3 tbsp sweet sherry or Madeira
2 tsp ground ginger
grated rind and juice of ½ orange
12oz ready-made puff pastry
egg or milk, to glaze
salt and black pepper

1 Place the carcasses and bones in a pan, with any giblets and half the onion, the bay leaves, carrots and black peppercorns. Cover with water and bring to the boil. Simmer until reduced to about 1¼ cups, then strain the stock, ready to use.

2 Cut the game meat into even size pieces. Fry the remaining onion, chopped, in the oil until softened. Then add the bacon and meat and fry quickly to seal. Sprinkle on the flour and stir until beginning to brown. Gradually add the stock, stirring as it thickens, then add the sherry or Madeira, ginger, orange rind and juice, and seasoning. Simmer for 20 minutes.

3 Transfer to a 3¾ cup pie dish and allow to cool slightly. Put a pie funnel in the centre of the filling to help hold up the pastry.

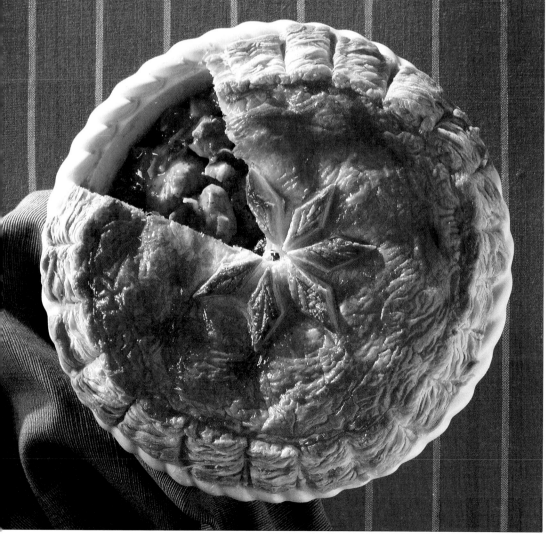

4 Preheat the oven to 425°F. Roll out the pastry to 1in larger than the dish. Cut off a ½in strip all round. Dampen the rim of the dish and press on the strip of pastry. Dampen again and then lift the pastry carefully over the pie, sealing the edges well at the rim. Trim off the excess pastry, use to decorate the top, then brush the pie with egg or milk.

5 Bake for 15 minutes, then reduce the heat to 375°F, for a further 25–30 minutes. Serve with red currant, or sage and apple, jelly.

Roast Chicken with Celery Root

INGREDIENTS

Serves 4
3½lb chicken
1 tbsp butter

For the stuffing
1lb celery root
2 tbsp butter
3 slices bacon, chopped
1 onion, finely chopped
leaves from 1 thyme sprig, chopped
leaves from 1 small tarragon sprig,
  chopped
2 tbsp chopped fresh parsley
1½ cups fresh brown bread crumbs
dash of Worcestershire sauce
1 egg
salt and black pepper

1 To make the stuffing, cook the celery root in boiling water until tender. Drain well and chop finely.

2 Heat the butter in a saucepan, then gently cook the bacon and onion until the onion is soft. Stir the celery root and herbs into the pan and cook, stirring occasionally, for 2–3 minutes. Meanwhile, preheat the oven to 400°F.

COOK'S TIP

Roll any excess stuffing into small balls and bake in an ovenproof dish with the chicken for about 20–30 minutes until golden brown.

3 Remove the pan from the heat and stir in the fresh bread crumbs, Worcestershire sauce, seasoning and sufficient egg to bind. Use to stuff the neck end of the chicken. Season the bird's skin, then rub with the butter.

4 Roast the chicken, basting occasionally with the juices, for 1¼–1½ hours, until the juices run clear when the thickest part of the leg is pierced.

5 Turn off the oven, prop the door open slightly and allow the chicken to rest for 10 minutes before carving.

Chicken, Carrot and Leek Parcels

These intriguing parcels may sound a bit fussy for everyday, but they take very little time and you can freeze them – ready to cook gently from frozen.

INGREDIENTS

Serves 4
4 chicken fillets or boneless breast
  portions
2 small leeks, sliced
2 carrots, grated
4 pitted black olives, chopped
1 garlic clove, crushed
1–2 tbsp olive oil
8 anchovy fillets
salt and black pepper
black olives and herb sprigs, to garnish

1 Preheat the oven to 400°F. Season the chicken well.

2 Divide the leeks equally among four sheets of greased wax paper, about 9in square. Place a piece of chicken on top of each.

3 Mix the carrots, olives, garlic and oil together. Season lightly and place on top of the chicken portions. Top each with two of the anchovy fillets, then carefully wrap up each parcel, making sure the paper folds are underneath and the carrot mixture on top.

4 Bake for 20 minutes and serve hot, in the paper, garnished with black olives and herb sprigs.

Chicken in a Tomato Coat

INGREDIENTS

Serves 4–6
3½– 4lb free-range chicken
1 small onion
1 tbsp butter
5 tbsp ready-made tomato sauce
2 tbsp chopped, mixed fresh herbs,
  such as parsley, tarragon, sage, basil
  and marjoram, or 2 tsp dried
small glass of dry white wine
2–3 small tomatoes, sliced
olive oil
little cornstarch (optional)
salt and black pepper

1 Preheat the oven to 375°F. Wash and wipe dry the chicken and place in a roasting pan. Place the onion, butter and a little salt and black pepper inside the chicken.

2 Spread most of the tomato sauce over the chicken and sprinkle with half the herbs and some seasoning. Pour the wine into the roasting pan.

3 Cover with foil, then roast for 1½ hours, basting occasionally. Remove the foil, spread with the remaining sauce and the sliced tomatoes and drizzle with oil. Continue cooking for a further 20–30 minutes, or until the chicken is cooked through.

4 Sprinkle the remaining herbs over the chicken, then carve into portions. Thicken the sauce with a little cornstarch if you wish. Serve hot.

Rabbit with Mustard

INGREDIENTS

Serves 4

1 tbsp flour
1 tbsp mustard powder
4 large rabbit joints
2 tbsp butter
2 tbsp oil
1 onion, finely chopped
⅔ cup beer
1¼ cups chicken or veal
   stock
1 tbsp tarragon vinegar
2 tbsp dark brown sugar
2–3 tsp mild mustard
salt and black pepper

To finish

4 tbsp butter
2 tbsp oil
1 cup fresh bread crumbs
1 tbsp snipped fresh chives
1 tbsp chopped fresh tarragon

1 Preheat the oven to 325°F. Mix the flour and mustard powder together, then put on a plate.

2 Dip the rabbit joints in the flour mixture, reserve excess flour. Heat the butter and oil in a heavy flameproof casserole, then brown the rabbit. Transfer to a plate. Stir in the onion and cook until soft.

3 Stir any reserved flour mixture into the casserole, cook for 1 minute, then stir in the beer, stock and vinegar. Bring to the boil and add the sugar and pepper. Simmer for 2 minutes.

4 Return the rabbit and any juices that have collected on the plate, to the casserole, cover tightly and cook in the oven for 1 hour.

5 Stir the prepared mustard and salt to taste into the casserole, cover again and cook over a low heat for a further 15 minutes.

6 To finish, heat together the butter and oil in a frying pan and fry the bread crumbs, stirring frequently, until golden, then stir in the herbs. Transfer the rabbit to a warmed serving dish, sprinkle over the bread crumb mixture and serve hot.

Turkey Hot-pot

INGREDIENTS

Serves 4

4oz kidney beans, soaked overnight
   and drained
3 tbsp butter
2 herby pork sausages
1lb turkey casserole meat
3 leeks, sliced
2 carrots, finely chopped
4 tomatoes, chopped
2–3 tsp tomato paste
bouquet garni
1⅔ cups chicken stock
salt and black pepper

1 Cook the beans in boiling water for 40 minutes, then drain well.

2 Meanwhile, heat the butter in a flameproof casserole, then cook the sausages until browned and the fat runs. Drain on kitchen paper, stir the turkey into the casserole and cook until lightly browned all over, then transfer to a bowl using a slotted spoon. Stir the leeks and carrot into the casserole and brown lightly.

3 Add the tomatoes and tomato paste and simmer gently for about 5 minutes.

4 Chop the sausages and return to the casserole with the beans, turkey, bouquet garni, stock and seasoning. Cover and cook gently for about 1¼ hours, until the beans are tender and there is very little liquid.

Moroccan Cornish Game Hens

INGREDIENTS 🍎

Serves 4

1½ cups cooked long grain rice
1 small onion, chopped finely
finely grated rind and juice of 1 lemon
2 tbsp chopped mint
3 tbsp chopped dried apricots
2 tbsp plain yogurt
2 tsp ground turmeric
2 tsp ground cumin
2 x 1lb Cornish game hens
salt and black pepper
lemon slices and mint sprigs, to garnish

1 Preheat the oven to 400°F. Mix together the rice, onion, lemon rind, mint, and apricots. Stir in half each of the lemon juice, yogurt, turmeric, cumin, and salt and pepper.

2 Stuff the hens with the rice mixture at the neck end only. Any spare stuffing can be served separately. Place the hens on a rack in a roasting pan.

3 Mix together the remaining lemon juice, yogurt, turmeric, and cumin, then brush this over the hens. Cover loosely with foil and roast in the oven for 30 minutes.

4 Remove the foil and roast for a further 15 minutes, or until golden brown and the juices run clear, not pink, when pierced.

5 Cut the hens in half with a sharp knife or poultry shears, and serve with the reserved rice. Garnish with lemon slices and fresh mint.

COOK'S TIP

If you aren't using leftover rice, but cooking it especially for this recipe, make sure the rice has cooled completely before adding to the other stuffing ingredients.

Sticky Ginger Chicken

INGREDIENTS 🍎

Serves 4

2 tbsp lemon juice
2 tbsp brown sugar
1 tsp grated fresh ginger root
2 tsp soy sauce
8 chicken drumsticks, skinned
black pepper

VARIATION

They are not as low in fat, but skinless duck breasts would be equally good in this recipe. Cook them until they are still very slightly pink in the center.

---

1 Mix together the lemon juice, sugar, ginger, soy sauce, and pepper.

2 With a sharp knife, slash the chicken drumsticks about three times through the thickest part, then toss the chicken in the glaze.

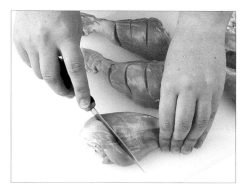

3 Cook the chicken under a broiler, or barbecue, turning occasionally and brushing with the glaze, until the chicken is golden and the juices run clear, not pink, when pierced. Serve on a bed of lettuce, with crusty bread.

Curried Chicken and Apricot Pie

This pie is unusually sweet-sour and very tasty. Use boneless turkey instead of chicken if you wish, or even some leftovers from a roast turkey – the dark, moist leg meat is best.

INGREDIENTS

Serves 6

2 tbsp sunflower oil
1 large onion, chopped
1lb boneless chicken, roughly chopped
1 tbsp curry paste or powder
2 tbsp apricot or peach chutney
⅔ cup ready-to-eat dried apricots, halved
1 cup cooked, sliced carrots
1 tsp mixed dried herbs
4 tbsp crème fraîche or sour cream
12oz ready-made pie crust
little egg or milk, to glaze
salt and black pepper

1 Heat the oil in a large pan and fry the onion and chicken until just coloring. Add the curry paste or powder and fry for 2 minutes more.

2 Add the chutney, apricots, carrots, herbs and crème fraîche or cream to the pan with seasoning. Mix together well and then transfer to a deep 4–5 cup ovenproof pie dish.

3 Roll out the pastry to 1in wider than the pie dish. Cut a strip of pastry from the edge. Dampen the rim of the dish, press on the strip, then brush these strips with water and place the sheet of pastry on top. Press to seal.

4 Preheat the oven to 375°F. Trim off any excess pastry and use to make an attractive pattern on the top if you wish. Brush all over with beaten egg or milk and bake for 40 minutes, until crisp and golden.

Cornish Game Hens with Raisin Stuffing

INGREDIENTS

Serves 4

1 cup port wine

⅔ cup raisins

1 tbsp walnut oil

3oz mushrooms, finely chopped

1 large celery stick, finely chopped

1 small onion, chopped

1 cup fresh white bread crumbs

½ cup chopped walnuts

1 tbsp each chopped fresh basil and
  parsley

½ tsp dried thyme

6 tbsp butter, melted

4 Cornish game hens

salt and black pepper

salad and cherry tomatoes, to serve

1 Preheat the oven to 350°F. Place the port and raisins in a bowl and soak for about 20 minutes.

2 Meanwhile, heat the oil in a frying pan. Add the mushrooms, celery, onion and ¼ tsp salt and cook over a low heat for 8–10 minutes, until softened. Leave to cool slightly.

3 Drain the raisins, reserving the port. Combine the raisins, bread crumbs, walnuts, basil, parsley and thyme in a large bowl. Stir in the mushroom and onion mixture and 4 tbsp of the butter. Add salt and pepper to taste.

4 Fill the cavity of each bird with the stuffing mixture. Do not pack down. Tie the legs together, looping the tail with string to enclose the stuffing.

5 Brush each bird with the remaining butter and place in a baking dish just large enough to hold the birds comfortably. Pour over the reserved port.

6 Roast for about 1 hour, basting occasionally. To test whether they are cooked, pierce the thigh with a skewer: the juices should run clear. Serve accompanied by salad and cherry tomatoes, with the cooking juices poured over each bird.

French-style Cornish Game Hens

INGREDIENTS

Serves 4

1 tbsp olive oil
1 onion, sliced
1 large garlic clove, sliced
½ cup diced lightly smoked bacon
2 Cornish game hens (just under
   1lb each)
2 tbsp butter, melted
2 baby celery hearts, each cut into 4
8 baby carrots
2 small zucchini, cut into chunks
8 small new potatoes
2½ cups chicken stock
⅔ cup dry white wine
1 bay leaf
2 fresh thyme sprigs
2 fresh rosemary sprigs
1 tbsp butter, softened
1 tbsp flour
salt and black pepper
fresh herbs, to garnish

1 Preheat the oven to 375°F. Heat the olive oil in a large flameproof casserole and add the onion, garlic and bacon. Sauté for 5–6 minutes, until the onion has softened.

2 Brush the hens with a little of the melted butter and season well. Lay on top of the onion mixture and arrange the prepared vegetables around them. Pour the chicken stock and wine around the birds and add the herbs.

3 Cover, bake for 20 minutes, then remove the lid and brush the birds with the remaining butter. Bake for a further 25–30 minutes until golden.

4 Transfer the hens to a warmed serving platter and cut each in half with poultry shears or scissors. Remove the vegetables with a slotted spoon and arrange them round the birds. Cover with foil and keep warm.

5 Discard the herbs from the pan juices. In a bowl mix together the butter and flour to form a paste. Bring the liquid in the pan to a boil and then whisk in teaspoonfuls of the paste until thickened. Season the sauce and serve with the hens and vegetables, garnished with fresh herbs.

Coq au Vin

INGREDIENTS

Serves 4

3 tbsp flour
3lb chicken, cut into 8 pieces
1 tbsp olive oil
4 tbsp butter
20 baby onions
3oz piece of slab bacon without rind,
  diced
about 20 button mushrooms
2 tbsp brandy
1 bottle red Burgundy wine
bouquet garni
3 garlic cloves
1 tsp soft light brown sugar
1 tbsp butter, softened
1 tbsp flour
salt and black pepper
1 tbsp chopped fresh parsley and
  croûtons, to garnish

1 Place the flour and seasoning in a large plastic bag and shake each chicken piece in it until lightly coated. Heat the oil and butter in a large flameproof casserole. Add the onions and bacon and sauté for 3–4 minutes, until the onions have browned lightly. Add the mushrooms and fry for 2 minutes. Remove with a slotted spoon, place in a bowl and reserve.

2 Add the chicken pieces to the hot oil and cook until browned on all sides, about 5–6 minutes. Pour in the brandy and (standing well back from the pan) carefully light it with a match, then shake the pan gently until the flames subside. Pour on the wine, add the bouquet garni, garlic, sugar and seasoning.

3 Bring to a boil, cover and simmer for 1 hour, stirring occasionally. Return the reserved onions, bacon and mushrooms to the casserole, cover and cook for a further 30 minutes.

4 Lift out the chicken, vegetables and bacon with a slotted spoon and arrange on a warmed dish.

5 Remove the bouquet garni and boil the liquid rapidly for 2 minutes to reduce slightly. Cream the butter and flour together and whisk in teaspoonfuls of the mixture until the liquid has thickened slightly. Pour this sauce over the chicken and serve garnished with parsley and croûtons.

INDEX